ENTREPRENEURIAL MANAGEMENT

ENTREPRENEURIAL MANAGEMENT

New Technology and New Market Development

Edited by

KENNETH D. WALTERS

BALLINGER PUBLISHING COMPANY
Cambridge, Massachusetts
A Subsidiary of Harper & Row, Publishers, Inc.

International Standard Book Number: 0-88730-266-1

Library of Congress Catalog Card Number: 88-31239

Printed in the United States of America

Library of Congress Cataloging-in-Publication Data

Entrepreneurial management : new technology and new market
  development / edited by Kenneth D. Walters.
    p.   cm.
  Includes bibliographies and index.
  ISBN 0-88730-266-1
  1. High technology industries—United States—Management—Case
studies.   2. Technological innovations—United States—Management—
Case studies.   3. Entrepreneurship—United States—Case studies.
4. Competition, International—Case studies.   I. Walters, Kenneth D.
HD62.37.E58   1989
338'.06—dc19   88-31239
                                                                    CIP

CONTENTS

LIST OF FIGURES AND TABLES

ACKNOWLEDGMENTS

A number of dedicated and resourceful people and organizations helped make this book possible.

Ronya Kozmetsky, president of the RGK Foundation, combines a profound belief in the importance of business education for men and women with an entrepreneurial enthusiasm for new ventures and creative approaches to problem-solving. Without her encouragement and dedication, the book would not have been possible.

Dr. George Kozmetsky, director of the IC² Institute at the University of Texas, Austin, and chairman of the RGK Foundation, personifies those rare qualities that make him a seminal thinker in management education: strategic vision, extraordinary perception of new developments, and commitment to ever better business theories and management practices. Dr. Kozmetsky played an invaluable role in planning the book.

A student coordinating team from the School of Business at California Polytechnic State University managed the conference upon which this book is based. The creative duo who displayed resourcefulness and flair in solving problems efficiently was Keith Eggleton and Kara Smith, business students at Cal Poly.

Thanks go to Cal Poly President Warren J. Baker and Senior Vice President for Academic Affairs Malcolm W. Wilson for their strong support of the conference and interest in interdisciplinary research and education in business and engineering.

I also wish to thank Roger Dunbar and Steven Burrill of Arthur Young International for their support and encouragement, and I appreciate the financial support of Arthur Young, which cosponsored the conference.

The School of Business at Cal Poly is indebted to the RGK Foundation for its willingness to support education in entrepreneurial management, as manifested in so many ways, including its sponsorship of the conference.

Dr. Raymond Smilor, executive director of the IC^2 Institute, deserves my deep thanks for his critical role in the program planning and in the preparation of this book. Dr. Smilor's intelligence, cheerfulness, and willingness to share his expertise and insights are greatly appreciated.

Margery Harris of the Cal Poly School of Business deserves special thanks for her unfailing dedication, hard work, and multiple skills in managing hundreds of details with perpetual courtesy and resourcefulness in preparing for the conference and in preparing the manuscript for this book. She was ably assisted by Melody DeMeritt, who also devoted many long hours to the success of the conference and this book.

Finally, I appreciate the assistance of Marjorie Richman of Ballinger in the preparation of the manuscript. She has been an outstanding and helpful individual with whom to work.

INTRODUCTION
Entrepreneurial Management and New Technology

Kenneth D. Walters

Managers of both small and large American firms keenly realize that global competition, especially from Asian nations, is becoming more and more intense. The underlying causes for the United States' inability to maintain its leadership in the world marketplace are broad, diffuse, and complex. They permeate nearly every aspect of the nation's economy and social system. But it is not as if the United States lacks vitally important advantages and resources. U.S. science and technology are still preeminent in most basic fields of knowledge. The challenge ahead is not primarily scientific or technological; it is managerial. Global competition poses a challenge to American institutions' ability to coordinate their energies and activities. This requires a new vision and new managerial approaches—what Peter Drucker calls "entrepreneurial management."

THE COMPETITIVENESS CRISIS

Innovative technology applications—new high-quality products, processes, and services—are increasingly manufactured and marketed, as well as financed more rapidly and more efficiently, by companies located outside the United States. Foreign-based firms have strong support systems from their private and public sector infrastructures and follow different strategies and policies than most U.S. firms. They target leading economic sectors and technologies that promise the greatest growth in the years ahead. Semiconductors, machine tools, robots, telecommunications, biotechnology, advanced materials, fiber optics — these technologies have been earmarked for special attention and assistance. Societal institutions rally around the goal of economic growth through technology commercialization.

Understanding the nature of the growing international competition for high-technology-related markets must become a priority for those preparing for management in the global economy in the 1990s and the twenty-first century. How do firms capture high-tech markets? What technological and managerial innovations are responsible for individual successes in the fiercely competitive environment faced by business today?

Only within the past decade has the new international competition shocked us into questioning whether the traditional methods of managing technology commercialization are adequate. The fact that the United States has lost major manufacturing sectors, one after another, to Asian superiority has finally begun to focus some attention on the problem. Why does the United States no longer control world markets — except in its role as consumer? How did this happen? How can we possess world-class scientific talent and yet lose high-tech industrial leadership? How is industrial leadership in high-tech regained? Are we destined to become "a farm" — as some Japanese commentators have derisively referred to the U.S. economy?

The need for a national agenda to deal with the declining American competitiveness was spelled out by the President's Commission on Industrial Competitiveness — the first major public document to strongly sound a warning of the alarming trends. The continuing erosion has spawned a new generation of studies and reports from government, business, and the academic community. Congress has held numerous hearings to study new legislation to address the problem.

The recent studies by the Office of Technology Assessment (OTA) emphasize that new technologies are a major force in reshaping the U.S. economy and society. Technology is transforming the American economy in ways that are "likely to reshape every product, every science, and every job in the United States." The OTA report is but the latest in a series of reports that soberly point out that our future national standard of living and position in the world economy rest on making the right choices in recognizing technology's role in economic change and managing technology wisely for economic growth, national pride, and security.

The new competition from abroad — and the U.S. response to it — poses the single most important challenge to management since World War II. In the United States, greater emphasis must be placed on the critical role of management in the global competition to develop and exploit new technologies. A major entrepreneurial opportunity for management will be to develop new ways to manage emerging collaborative relationships creatively and effectively.

MANAGEMENT AND TECHNOLOGY

As the chapters in this book show, the United States is not without successful case studies of entrepreneurial management of high-tech institutions. Managers in many American organizations are rising to this challenge. Management functions and thinking are changing as a result of new technologies and the new global competition, proving that American management can alter its vision, its style, and its ability to compete. Creative and innovative managers can be found in the universities, in the federal labs, in large established companies, and in new emerging firms. The traditional styles of managing, which often reflect the traditional thinking in American business schools, are just beginning to give way to fresh approaches in marketing, finance, operations, production, legal affairs, organizational behavior, and organizational design.

Entrepreneurial management pulls together capital, intellectual resources, and technology to create new ventures and to revitalize existing enterprises. The task is to take these components and add value to them, thereby providing new or better products and services. Entrepreneurship starts with ideas and transforms them into realities. Entrepreneurs are forces of energy, change, creativity, and dynamism. They are driven to do new things or to do old things in better ways.

Entrepreneurial management is concerned with new ideas, directions, relationships, concepts, methods, and modes of operation. Special attention is given to strategies that create competitive advantages.

Entrepreneurship is the single most important factor in stimulating a vital private sector, creating jobs, and encouraging competitiveness and economic growth. Moreover, entrepreneurial management in large existing companies is also a key element in the competitiveness strategy for the United States in the world marketplace.

This book is a series of case studies and analyses of entrepreneurial management in high-technology industries and institutions. To be sure, entrepreneurial management does not only exist in high technology; in fact, some of the most entrepreneurial managers and companies are in low-tech or no-tech environments — and, indeed, high-tech organizations can lack entrepreneurial management.

But, as the following chapters reveal, the high-tech environment is a fertile ground for the evolution and cultivation of entrepreneurial management. The essence of the high-tech business venture is innovation and application of new technology. This is typically characterized by new products, new markets, new production methods, new marketing methods, new financial approaches, and new ways of motivating and organizing people. As George Kozmetsky states in Chapter 17, "Emerging industries are the drivers for determining a new approach to management, if we are to maintain preeminence scientifically and economically. Entrepreneurial managers must be more creative and innovative than today's traditional professional managers or today's entrepreneurs."

Emerging high-tech industries tend to evolve entrepreneurial approaches to management as new challenges are faced — sometimes successfully and sometimes unsuccessfully. Just to survive, high-tech managers face special pressures to respond to and cope with rapid change in technology and in markets. They are not usually given much time in which to do so.

This book includes chapters by entrepreneurial managers in three kinds of organizations: large established companies, new high-tech firms, and public sector institutions. The need today is for managers who can expand the art of entrepreneurship in all three types of organizations. We are leaving behind the stable period in which it was often sufficient for organizations to perform routine tasks and serve stable markets. The entrepreneurial managers of tomorrow must be able to understand and manage in a far more dynamic, complex, and fast-paced environment.

Managers are needed who know more about technology. Transforming science into technological resources has traditionally been the task of scientists and engineers. Increasingly, however, there is greater demand for entrepreneurial managers who can integrate technology with business markets and needs. Individuals schooled in business and engineering or business and the sciences are needed to start new companies and to strengthen and expand existing firms.

A further task of managers is to understand the depth of the challenges of the global marketplace and competition in technology-based industries. Managers must understand the economic and political causes and consequences of global flows of technology and capital. Why is the United States awash in the capital pouring from Japan into the United States and indeed the entire world? Managers should comprehend the strategies by which other nations' industries are organized and managed. To appreciate how future economic growth requires linking the scientific and technical establishment with the financial and industrial sectors is a central task of entrepreneurial management.

ENTREPRENEURIAL MANAGEMENT

This book shows how managers in diverse organizations are responding to the challenge of intense competition. Entrepreneurial management in a high-tech environment with rapidly changing markets and technologies deals with a number of issues that are repeatedly emphasized in the following chapters. These issues are discussed below.

New Linkages with Organizations and Institutions

Entrepreneurial managers in high technology are reaching out and linking up with other organizations in their drive for competitive advantage and commercial opportunities. Firms are developing closer ties to universities as a source of research and technology and as a means of monitoring new developments on a continuing basis (see chapters by Michael Bandler, Alvin Kwiram, Debra Amidon Rogers, and Ronald Rosemeier). New institutions are linking increased corporate support for university research with university programs to orient research capabilities toward industry's needs. Mutual interests and compatibilities are increasing. In Chapter 2, Kwiram discusses the development of the Center for Process Analytical Chemistry at the University of Washington — one example of an extraordinary, entrepreneurial relationship that applies a major university's research capabilities to industry's interest and needs. The creation of consortia, such as the Microelectronics and Computer Technology Corporation (MCC), which John Pinkston discusses in Chapter 14, is a further strong indication that firms can no longer "go it alone" in R&D. New technologies are so complex that no single company can do all the research or exploit a substantial share of the market applications and opportunities that exist (see Chapter 17 by Kozmetsky). The federal laboratories, long known for their specific mission orientation, are making their technologies available to universities and to industry (see Chapter 16 by Eugene Stark).

In short, entrepreneurial managers are keenly sensing an expanding opportunity to reach out and build innovative strategic ties, leveraging their own assets with the critical elements of talent, capital, ideas, and managerial know-how found in other institutions. Successful commercialization demands a great increase in collaboration and cooperation between businesses and public sector institutions. As Kozmetsky points out, three groups of people – those who create technology, those who create markets, and those who use technology – must pool their efforts to achieve more rapid commercialization of the nation's scientific and technological resources.

An Entrepreneurial Organization Design

Just as new links between organizations open up new opportunities and create synergies, so also do new ties between specialists and departments within organizations. As Herbert Boyer of Genentech notes in Chapter 3, entrepreneurial skills, managerial skills, and technological skills must be combined at an early stage to accelerate commercialization of a new technology. Furthermore, scientists and engineers in established companies, who have traditionally prided themselves on doing specialized research in relative isolation, are more closely coordinating their efforts with other experts in the organization.

Several contributors suggest that successful technological innovations are spawned by teams of people from such diverse areas as finance, marketing, operations, legal, and R&D – together assessing and coordinating new markets with new technologies. Bandler points out, in Chapter 10, how introductions of major new technologies at Pacific Bell are fostered by a team approach involving many departments in the company. In Chapter 12, Charles Shorter credits TRW's successful commercialization of defense technologies to a project team drawn from both the business and the technical sides of TRW. Klaus Dahl from Raychem, in Chapter 7 states that "R&D divorced from manufacturing, marketing, and selling, tends to produce stillborn babies."

Technology innovation should have the commitment of everyone involved — the "receivers" of the technology as well as the "senders", Pinkston suggests. In Shorter's words, "Technology must be packaged with market research, prototypes, manufacturing, sales, distribution, training, and maintenance." The purpose is not only coordination and information; it is to develop a market-driven focus and attitude by all groups in the organization.

Successful strategy in high technology is two-fold: to create business goals based on the potential of the new technology, and to create technology goals based on the business opportunities. Both of these goals — markets and technology — are moving targets, and people from each of the "two cultures" of business and technology must closely and continuously coordinate efforts in order to achieve optimal results.

The Entrepreneurial Culture

Setting an entrepreneurial tone and establishing an innovative value system in the organization are critical factors of successful entrepreneurial management. Bandler describes how an "innovative spirit" was essential to respond to new market needs in the fast-changing telecommunications market. According to James Woolley (Chapter 9), among 3M's basic tenets are the policies of never blaming a person for an error resulting from honest effort, and "taking care of" (protecting and rewarding) innovators. He adds that 3M's entire corporate culture is built on new products and continuous innovation, requiring a "demanding, yet nurturing" management. Just as employees are encouraged to innovate and are not punished when a project fails, equally important is 3M's "celebration of successes."

Corporate culture is partially determined by the qualities of the people it recruits. Boyer notes that Genetech "needed to attract the brightest young scientists we could find," and succeeded by promising them the freedom to publish their research results, even though this could conflict with a firm's need for proprietary information. In Chapter 4, Kathleen Wiltsey states that stock options and financial incentives were used at Amgen to attract scientific talent. She adds: "People joke that in biotech companies, the assets walk out the door at the end of the day."

Rosemeier states that in a high-tech company, "one can hardly overestimate the importance of getting the best people." His policy of hiring people willing to take risks was achieved in the time-honored American tradition of hiring new immigrants:

> When I first started the company, I had a very hard time getting Americans who would want to take a risk with a company offering very low-paying jobs. I had no problem getting immigrants. My three top people were immigrants who had come to the United States with two garbage bags of clothes and old suitcases. These are people who left their countries, broke family ties, and came to this country with nothing. These are risk-takers. There are Americans like that also — of whom we have the best — but it is difficult to find them.

Close Customer Interface

Successful technology commercialization marries a new technology to a need. In the technology transfer literature this is sometimes referred to as the "market pull" theory of technology transfer — the market discovers or motivates the creation of the technology. In Chapter 6, Gilman notes that in the advanced materials revolution now occurring, profiles of user needs are becoming the basic drivers of change. The suitability of materials for a particular task is the major factor in the current development of major new materials. Consumer need is the starting point in the search for new technology.

Bandler confirms that technology should be viewed as a solution to customer needs, not as an end in itself. In Shorter's words, "The customer buys benefits, not technology."

In Chapter 11, E. Oran Brigham makes the fundamental point that new technology can succeed in the marketplace, where it either lowers costs, adds benefits to customers, or does both. More costly new technologies, such as gallium arsenide-based products developed at Avantek, succeed when they provide added value to justify the increased cost. He adds that market segments should be selected so that a company's technology places it in an innovative and leadership position — a point also stressed by Rosemeier.

A high-tech research lab such as SRI International stays in touch with consumer needs by its "Business Consulting Group," according to Richard Marciano (see Chapter 13). The group maintains contacts with industry people who have product-line responsibility, and communicates those needs back to the scientific-technical staff at SRI.

Dahl reports an innovative strategy at Raychem of involving large "lead customers" in the development of new technology. These large customers work closely with Raychem in refining the new technology to their specific needs, sharing the costs and risks.

A New Model for Economic Development

As Kozmetsky and Kwiram point out, a new model or paradigm is emerging to deal with economic development and technology commercialization. The formidable investment in basic research that the United States has made since World War II curiously has not been accompanied by an explicit strategy for commercialization. Commercialization has been haphazard and uncoordinated. The traditional view was that basic research would automatically "trickle down" to individuals and companies. Commercialization of new technology was taken for granted. Little thought was given to precisely how science became technology, how technology was transformed into new industries, and how this process could be catalyzed and managed better. It was assumed that the process did not need to be managed.

The new paradigm for technology commercialization and economic development departs from the traditional view that universities, businesses, and governmental units should be antiseptically compartmentalized from each other and the individual missions of each pursued in an insular environment. The new model recognizes the need for strategic cooperation between institutions, focusing on the vital role of world-class scientific research and technological leadership in promoting economic growth and diversification. It emphasizes the need to leverage the national investment in basic science with the resources of industry, capital, and the public sector to build a higher standard of living, economic security, and public benefit. International competition is not only for Nobel prizes but for the new industries and new wealth that emerge from commercialization of science and technology. New and more innovative institutions must be devised to accelerate technology commercialization.

Technology and Strategy

The chapters that follow show that new technologies are dramatically changing the structure and strategy of industry in the most advanced industrial nations. Perhaps the most widely recognized of these changes is that in information technology; the information industry touches virtually all other industries. Based on the computer and its associated paraphernalia, the information industry is causing a revolution in the availability of knowledge critical for competitive business decisions. We are seeing the beginning of large sets of integrated computerized data and knowledge bases that aid in decisionmaking, as the chapter by Shorter shows. The acquisition and interpretation of information will undergird competitive industrial strategy.

A second revolution, closely related to the information explosion, is in telecommunications. With information comes the need to transport that information to billions of users—the need for technologies of dissemination. Service and cost are the two major drivers of the market and of new technology. In his chapter, Brigham outlines a number of new markets that new telecommunications technology promises to open in the near future.

Another revolution—usually overlooked or underappreciated—is occurring in advanced materials. The basic shift is from commodity materials toward materials designed to fit the needs of each particular job and consumer, as Gilman demonstrates. The chapters by Dahl, Rosemeier, and Woolley show the incredibly diverse markets where new advanced materials are having major impacts. The future will be fast-paced, extremely competitive, and rewarding for entrepreneurial companies specializing in advanced materials.

The fourth revolution—potentially the most dramatic of all—is occurring in biotechnology. Although we are just at the beginning of this new era, the existing industries of pharmaceuticals, agriculture, and energy may never be the same.

The rapid development and commercialization of these new technologies in the 1990s and into the twenty-first century promise to alter factories, offices, retail establishments, and living patterns, and, indeed, the strategies of management.

A Global Focus

The business homilies "know thy customer" and "watch thy competitor" take on special meaning when the market is not only domestic but international. No nation's markets are completely insulated from what is happening in other countries. The emergence of the global economy is transforming the meaning of market research. The market is the world, and American managers need to know what is happening throughout the world.

Every high-tech industry faces present or potential challenges from abroad. In biotechnology, G. Steven Burrill (Chapter 5) notes that Japanese and European competition promises to be strong and well-financed. In advanced materials, Dahl reports that "more competition is on the horizon. In the 1990s we expect to see a number of additional manufacturers in the United States, Japan, and Europe." Rogers warns, in Chapter 1, of the newest Japanese industrial policy to transform Japan from a nation of "imitators" into "innovators." Through a "technopolis strategy," Japanese leaders have charted a comprehensive plan to modernize mature industries while concurrently developing high-tech innovation and manufacturing centers throughout Japan in all the key high-tech sectors. "There is no such system within the United States that so effectively integrates new knowledge into the mainstream of our economy," Rogers concludes.

On a positive note, American companies — Raychem and 3M are but two examples — can still set standards for the world. Dahl's advice from Raychem's perspective is to "go international, but retain a strong domestic market." Woolley notes that one of the prime managerial tenets at 3M is "the perspective of a global economy with the opportunity and need for participation in worldwide markets."

Patient Urgency

In high-tech industries, the time it takes to get a product to market is often the difference between success and failure.

The pressure to develop new products before competitors can do so is keen in high-tech industries. Several chapters deal with this problem and offer suggestions:

Japanese companies believe in pooling their resources and technical knowledge early in the research process. Rogers explains that this avoids duplication, conserves organizational resources, and rapidly disseminates research findings.

3M adheres to a policy of "patient urgency," according to Woolley. Patience is required because technological progress can be tedious and unpredictable, with many blind alleys. But urgency is also needed since the competitive advantage of developing new products faster than other firms is enormous.

Dahl points out that some technology developments are clearly long-term in nature. He credits Raychem's success, in part, on its willingness to invest in long-term projects that may achieve no rapid payback but are major innovations for long-term profitability.

Bandler notes that commercialization of major technological breakthroughs (such as fiber optics) requires a lengthy phase-in time and a major investment. A long-term technology strategy is required, but with an implementation policy to bring the technology to the market in stages.

Innovation in Public Sector Organizations

Innovation in public sector organizations is critical to successful technology commercialization. Public sector initiatives can leverage private sector resources and promote economic growth, thereby benefitting individuals, firms, and the general welfare. A number of innovative policies by public sector management are described in some detail in this book.

Kwiram describes how the Center for Process Analytical Chemistry (CPAC) was formed at the University of Washington, enabling sophisticated chemical instrumentation methods to be made more applicable and cost-effective to industry. The implications for quality control are profound. Entrepreneurial management at the University of Washington saw the need for a new organization, CPAC, to link the university's research resources with industrial applications. The

CPAC has developed a world-class reputation that embellishes the academic reputation of the university as well as benefitting industry and society.

In Chapter 15, Robert Gavin spells out the steps taken in the development of the University of Michigan's technology licensing office. The innovative strategy followed at that university made service to the university research community first priority, while assisting business and generating revenue were secondary priorities. The implementation of this strategy shows how a major university's research resources can foster collaborative and nurturing academic-community relationships.

Marciano describes how SRI International has adopted a variety of entrepreneurial approaches to move its technologies to the marketplace. There has been a definite movement toward greater entrepreneurship at SRI International, and new innovative methods of creating ownership rights in a nonprofit organization's technologies have been devised. One notable example is the royalty-sharing policy specifying that SRI's inventors can share in the entrepreneurial experience without having to leave the organization and set up their own firms.

Stark shows that the federal laboratories, prodded by the Stevenson-Wydler Act of 1980, are currently engaged in many entrepreneurial activities to commercialize their technology. Although we are only seeing the beginning of such efforts, the examples Stark provides are impressive.

The unifying theme throughout these chapters is that the opportunities for technology commercialization through entrepreneurial management are enormous and growing.

I THE TECHNOLOGY CHALLENGE TO MANAGEMENT

1 ENTREPRENEURIAL APPROACHES TO ACCELERATE TECHNOLOGY COMMERCIALIZATION

Debra M. Amidon Rogers

In the study by the National Research Council entitled "Management of Technology: The Hidden Competitive Advantage," the authors define how "the current, intensely competitive global environment is demanding a renewed emphasis on effective technology management and a reevaluation of traditional techniques."[1]

They describe in detail the roots of the problem and offer a "problem-driven" research agenda, which calls for an increased role for the National Science Foundation (NSF), the Department of Defense, and the National Aeronautics and Space Agency (NASA) in promoting public awareness and financing cross-disciplinary research on the subject. Identified industry needs include:

1. How to integrate technology into the overall strategic objectives of the firm
2. How to get into and out of technologies faster and more efficiently
3. How to assess/evaluate technology more effectively
4. How best to accomplish technology transfer
5. How to reduce new product development time
6. How to manage large, complex, and interdisciplinary or interorganizational projects/systems
7. How to manage the organization's internal use of technology
8. How to leverage the effectiveness of technical professionals

This is no small agenda!

3

THE INTERNATIONAL CONTEXT

These timely recommendations come in the midst of what some might describe as an awakening of America to the realities (and threats) of a global economy. Others, like Daniel Greenberg, editor of *Science and Government Report*, describe the scenario a bit more graphically:

> In its dedication to national security, the Reagan Administration has taken an extremely narrow view of what's threatening our security and the role that research and development must play in assuring our security. The fact is that we are leaving no stone unturned in seeking the means — through research and development — to confront the Soviet military threat. But, as real as that threat may be, what's rocking this country today is an attack — and it's not coming from the Soviet Union. It's coming from Japan, which takes the business of economic competition with us as seriously as we take the business of military competition with the Soviets.[2]

Greenberg is only one of many who question the current allocation of national resources in light of significant strides made recently by our foreign competitors in building R&D infrastructures that rival our own capacity to harness technical, human, and business resources for economic gain.

Take, for example, the newest Japanese industrial policy, which is intended to transform the nation of scientific "imitators" into "innovators," causing a fundamental shift in philosophy from "copying" to "creativity." Through a six-pronged "technopolis Strategy," Japanese leaders plan to create nineteen ultramodern Silicon Valleys throughout their country by the year 2000.[3] This plan calls for modernizing sunset industries, creating a balance between private industry and government, and strengthening regional economies through the planned development of high-tech centers.

Coupled with this aggressive approach is a belief that by pooling their resources and technical knowledge early in the research process, Japanese companies are able to advance the state of the art of technology. Research studies are unified and shared widely within the country. In his paper, "Technology Transfer and Cooperative Research in Japan," Thomas W. Eager, an MIT professor, describes how this strategy avoids unnecessary duplication, ensures efficient and effective allocation of industrial resources, and results in the rapid dissemination of new research findings.[4] There is no such system within the United States that so effectively integrates new knowledge into the mainstream of our economy.

The most striking example of the dichotomy between U.S. and Japanese approaches appeared in a Wall Street Journal article on the Japanese race to commercialize superconductors. "Four days after the Houston bombshell, Japan's Science and Technology Agency announced its intent to form a research consortium of Japanese companies, universities, and government labs. A week later the consortium was in place, including such industrial giants as NEC, Toshiba Corporation, Nippon Steel Corporation, and Mitsubishi Corporation."[5]

Although scientists in America (and abroad for that matter) may argue about how premature commercialization techniques might be, the story is illustrative of how readily the Japanese are willing (and able) to cooperatively capitalize on such a technological breakthrough. Response by America has been modest in comparison. The *Wall Street Journal* article notes that, by contrast, there is no nationally coordinated drive for capitalizing on the research findings.

NEED FOR A NEW SHARED VISION

In testimony given to the House Committee on Science and Technology, Lee W. Rivers stated that the time is past for studying industrial competitiveness:

> We do not need more studies, we do not need more finger-pointing or fault-finding—we do need a national consensus that industrial competitiveness is essential to the key role each can play in the step-by-step process of regaining America's position of leadership in the global marketplace.[6]

A new research action agenda is needed that focuses on the transfer of knowledge across disciplines, across sectors, across industries, across the profit and not-for-profit organizations. This new agenda will have to transcend our current thinking and serve as a catalyst for establishing a new vision of cooperative alliances. To that end, I offer the following planning model for discussion.

The process of harnessing creativity toward profitable innovation is a complex phenomenon. There are numerous players and factors

Figure 1–1.   Planning Model.

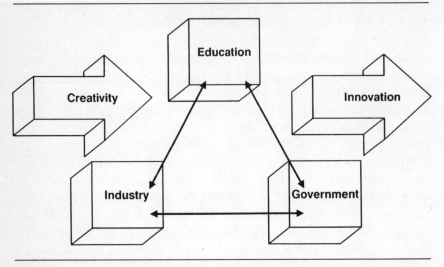

Source: Debra M. Amidon Rogers, "The Collective Challenge: Optimizing the Technology Alliance," in *Managing the Knowledge Asset into the 21st Century: Focus on Research Consortia* (Cambridge, Mass.: Technology Strategy Group, 1988) pp. 14–27.

involved that either hinder or enhance the process. Add to the scenario the three integral partners in the research enterprise — each with its own vision and paradigm — and ensuring mutual cooperative activity is a seemingly impossible task.

In order to analyze the strengths and weaknesses of the existing research infrastructure, there are at least three elements worthy of attention: structural issues, resource issues, and methods/tools available. At the core of the assessment is the viability of competitive technology transfer processes, which enable the profitable movement of knowledge through the three stages of innovation, as defined by Bruce Merryfield: I-Invention, II-Translation, and III-Commercialization.[7]

It is well known that the United States has maintained a leadership position in the creation of new knowledge. Nick Paleologos, a Massachusetts state representative, returned from a trip to Japan and, while commenting on our notable ability to produce 135 Nobel laureates, in contrast to Japan's four, observed that we fail miserably in managing the process of taking that creativity to the marketplace.

With this in mind, I have been working with the Technology Transfer Society, based in Indianapolis, to redefine the problem as one of a management agenda. Dan Dimancescu (coauthor of *The New*

Figure 1–2. Model Analysis.

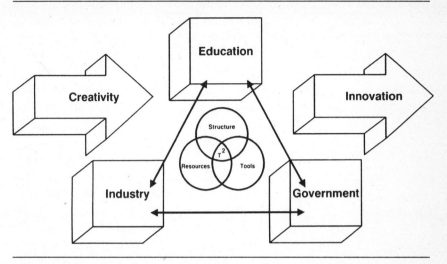

Source: Debra M. Amidon Rogers, "The Collective Challenge: Optimizing the Technology Alliance," in *Managing the Knowledge Asset into the 21st Century: Focus on Research Consortia* (Cambridge, Mass.: Technology Strategy Group, 1988) pp. 14–27.

Alliance)[8] and I cochaired a Critical Issues Roundtable, on "Management of the Knowledge Asset into the Twenty-First Century." At the heart of the discussion were the models mentioned above and the participants represented the national R&D scientific leadership across the sectors. What transpired was intended to launch the National Campaign for Competitive Technology Transfer, which was formally announced in Washington, D.C. in June 1987.

AN INSIDE VIEW OF DIGITAL TECHNOLOGY TRANSFER

The Digital External Research Program (ERP) has been in existence for over ten years. Only in the last few years, however, has structured attention been given to planning and technology transfer activities designed to optimize and leverage research results from external research laboratories, across the corporation.

Organizationally, we are part of Corporate Research and Architecture, the research arm of Digital's engineering/manufacturing organization. ERP is a worldwide program with bases in Geneva, Switzerland, and Hudson, Massachusetts; plans are also under way to hire someone in our R&D facility in Tokyo, Japan. The program is designed to augment in-house research efforts to develop technologies that will be required five to ten years from now to maintain our international competitive position. Major internal research efforts include the Systems Research Center and the Western Research Laboratory, both in Palo Alto, California. We also have several engineers on-site at the Microelectronic and Computer Technology Corporation in Austin, Texas. Several other applied research and advanced development centers reside in Digital facilities around the world.

Over the years, and especially since 1981 (due in part to the R&D tax credit incentive), the ERP budget has increased rapidly. Equipment grants have been allocated for research projects across twelve key technology areas, from artificial intelligence to very large scale integration. Recently, we added an area from Management Systems Research because of the need to focus on "process" as well as on "product" design.

There have been approximately 240 individual projects funded at more than one hundred universities. These projects are primarily equipment allowances provided for specific research "deliverables" that are carefully defined in a research agreement. We also manage a series of campus-based programs, which are multiyear, multimillion-dollar investments at strategic research universities. In several of those cases (for example, Project Athena at MIT), Digital engineers are placed on-site. The key to the success of the program is the requirement that technical sponsors be aligned with all projects. They are responsible for allocating a 6 percent internal fee, which funds the administration of our office. More importantly, they assign technical resources to monitor the progress of the project and integrate research results, as desirable, into the group(s) most likely to benefit. The technical review of proposals is performed by the Sponsored Research Board, composed of advanced development engineers/managers in each technology area.

In 1984, it became clear that a more systematic approach to technology transfer was necessary to better manage the multiple research relationships funded through ERP. A strategic plan was developed that incorporated three major thrusts: planning, programs, and communications. What follows is a brief description of some of the techniques and approaches we have incorporated to manage the process more efficiently and effectively.

After considerable discussion, we have defined the technology transfer process as "the complex communication phenomenon involved in the flow of ideas about new materials, products, and processes from an R&D establishment through different stages to utilization." The charter of the technology transfer staff is to develop programs that will maximize our return on investment. Note that basic research results generally come in the form of prototypes, algorithms, and product ideas, generally a long way from products and/or applications.

There are numerous other definitions of technology transfer used within Digital. They range from computerizing Third World nations to transferring artificial intelligence techniques directly into the mainstream of major customers. It can also mean transferring research developments from one part of our corporation into advanced development groups within Engineering. Most of the focus of ERP, and of the concepts described in this chapter, is on the integration of external research results into our own product ideas to make us technologically competitive.

The thread of the technology transfer process continues through all phases of product development and market acceptance.

Whether we refer to bringing research ideas into the corporation, moving them within line engineering groups, or integrating products through the manufacturing process, the issues (and opportunities) are still the same. Digital even offers an extensive six-week training course in artificial intelligence for customer point-of-sale people. The last two days of that course are dedicated to organizing technology transfer techniques to ensure marketplace adaptation.

The above continuum is similar to a color spectrum. At each connect point in the transfer process, it is not clear when the transfer takes place. It is difficult to assign specific steps, stages, or metrics of success as a product or process moves through each cycle. This is a challenge for all functional managers.

Within External Research, the staff is not seen as responsible for transferring the technology itself. Rather, we provide opportunities and tools for internal advanced development engineers to benefit

Figure 1–3.   Technology Transfer Continuum — Rethinking the Alliance (1985–2005).

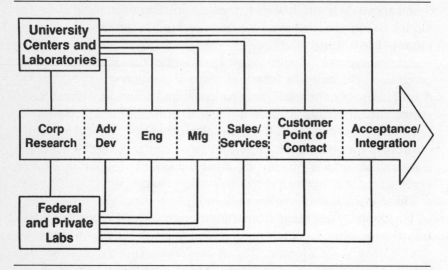

Source: Debra M. Amidon Rogers, "The Collective Challenge: Optimizing the Technology Alliance," in *Managing the Knowledge Asset into the 21st Century: Focus on Research Consortia* (Cambridge, Mass.: Technology Strategy Group, 1988) pp. 14–27.

from the knowledge and know-how of university researchers. Some sample activities include:

- As part of our strategic planning process, we have sponsored several studies and published internal technical reports to disseminate research findings. Examples include: analysis of the competition in the research community; analysis of the strengths and weaknesses of our technology transfer programs; identification of government-funded research opportunities.
- In June 1986 we brought together twenty-five engineering deans of the top research universities for a two-day technology exchange with senior Digital engineering management.
- We maintain relationships with over fifty affiliate programs or research centers. They can be institution-based (for example, the Center for Integrated Systems at Stanford) or consortial (such as Semiconductor Research Corporation [SRC]). Some are government-initiated, such as the NSF engineering research centers (for

example, the Center for Telecommunications Research at Columbia University).

- All grants, affiliate relationships and research center memberships require internal technical sponsorship. This is the critical link that ensures that the technology gets transferred into the line engineering organization.
- All the technical reports that we receive through research projects, affiliate programs, and customer visits are abstracted, keyworded, and made electronically available worldwide through our electronic Digital Library Network (DLN).
- In order to reach our sprawling research community, we developed an electronic videotex bulletin board, which includes research abstracts of all funded projects, profiles of our strategic research universities, competitive data, and relative research ranking.
- Throughout the year, Digital sponsors a series of roundtables, research forums and technical advisory panels on topics of particular interest to Digital engineers. Researchers are featured in any of the dozen internal Technical Seminar Series programs held on engineering facilities.

The ERP has evolved to such a degree that we are in the process of a new functional alignment that defines clear responsibilities, liaison relationships, and specific activities.

The new organization will have five components. The roles of Strategy, Operations, and Communications are not necessarily new. The Technology Exchange Program has the new mandate to build the infrastructure within Engineering and Manufacturing to receive the technology and know-how that Digital funds. Another new addition, Information Management Systems, could be the critical success factor for the coming year. Information is not the problem. Getting value-added information to those members of the internal technical community is the real challenge.

SIGNALS OF INCREASED EXTERNAL AWARENESS

One can hardly ignore the greater attention given to the technology transfer process and its role in technological innovation. At most

Figure 1–4.   Functional Alignment.

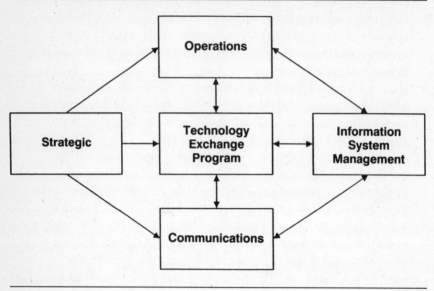

conferences that deal with university-industry-government interactions, discussions eventually shift to technology transfer, in most cases focusing on barriers rather than illuminating new strategies.

There are several activities under way that are worthy of note:

- The Technology Transfer Society, as mentioned above, launched its national campaign in June 1987 at its international symposium in Washington, D.C.
- The Semiconductor Research Corporation, with its sophisticated, electronic "information central," has established a technology transfer subcommittee of the Technical Advisory Board. In fact, Digital has commissioned a major study with SRC on how the Japanese transfer technology.
- The new Federal Technology Transfer Act is an attempt to structure the transference of modest funds (namely, 0.05 percent of budgets) of federal laboratories through the Federal Laboratory Consortium, which will be based at the National Bureau of Standards. This is intended to facilitate the acceleration of technology into the marketplace.

- The Industrial Research Institute (IRI), with its recent advanced study groups on technology transfer, offered the membership an opportunity to define how best to move research out of the laboratory and into the line organizations. The summary of those sessions highlights three elements of successful transfer: credibility (in other words, established track records); champion (that is, the need for someone to ride the process throughout or ensure that the baton is passed effectively); and continuous, value-added communications systems — formal or informal.
- The new Council on Research and Technology (CORETECH), an outgrowth of the Coalition for the Advancement of Industrial Technology, has established a technology transfer task force under its research policy committee.
- The National Center for Manufacturing Sciences, currently operating under the National Research Council, describes itself as a technology transfer vehicle for research across all manufacturing disciplines and industries.
- The Commission on Engineering and Technical Studies of the National Research Council sponsored a conference, based upon a proposal submitted by NASA, in June 1987 in Aspen, Colorado.

And I suspect that all this activity is only the beginning.

SUMMARY

As mentioned at the beginning of this presentation, there are many in this country who propose that we are indeed in a crisis situation. On several fronts, I am hard-pressed to argue. But note: half of the Japanese symbol for *crisis* represents the word *opportunity*. In fact, in their country, problems are perceived as opportunities to solve the problems.

Amidst the challenges of the technological age, the encroaching competitive threat, and the apparent fragmentation within our own research enterprise, there is a rethinking of our current values and practices. People in each sector appear more eager to be flexible and responsive to the challenge at hand. Quantum, rather than incremental, improvements will require some significant paradigm shifts in each sector — a movement toward a common vision. Dr. Paul Gray, president of MIT, describes it best:

Figure 1–5.   Japanese Symbol for Crisis.

Opportunity

Source: Debra M. Amidon Rogers, "The Collective Challenge: Optimizing the Technology Alliance," in *Managing the Knowledge Asset into the 21st Century: Focus on Research Consortia* (Cambridge, Mass.: Technology Strategy Group, 1988) pp. 14–27.

The creation of new products and services occurs when ideas, which may originate in basic research, are nurtured and developed in the context of actual needs and markets, when engineering virtuosity produces reliable, effective, and desirable products, and when the Congress, federal agencies, and corporations take the long view with regards to the value of basic research.[9]

It is clear that those corporations that successfully learn to manage the process of technology transfer may be able to maintain their competitive edge; for, in fact, that is precisely what those successful companies abroad appear to have achieved so effectively. This will require that the cultures of the three interdependent sectors become far more receptive to the transfer of knowledge throughout all stages of the process of innovation. Our resources, particularly technical leadership, will have to be more carefully utilized than ever before.

As Dr. Peter Bridenbaugh, Vice President for Research at Alcoa, once said, "Where we invest our intellectual capital and curiosity, technology transfer is not an issue."[10]

NOTES

1. Richie Herink, et al, *Management of Technology: The Hidden Competitive Advantage* (Washington, D.C.: National Academy Press, 1987) p. 5.
2. Daniel Greenberg, Major address for the Annual Conference of the National Council of University Research Administrators, November 1986.
3. Sheridan M. Tatsuno, *The Technopolis Strategy: Japan, High Technology, and the Control of the Twenty-First Century* (Englewood Cliffs, N.J.: Prentice-Hall, 1986).
4. Thomas W. Eager, "Technology Transfer and Cooperative Research in Japan," *Scientific Bulletin* (ONRFE) 10, no. 3 (1985).
5. Stephen Kreidler Yoder, "Japan Is Racing to Commercialize New Superconductors," *Wall Street Journal*, 20 March 1987.
6. Lee W. Rivers, "Time Is Past for Studying Industrial Competitiveness," *Research Management* 30, no. 1 (January-February 1987): p. 7.
7. D. Bruce Merryfield, "Forces of Change Affecting High Technology Industries," *National Journal*, 29 January 1983, p.253.
8. Dan Dimancescu and James Botkin, *The New Alliance: America's R&D Consortia*, (Cambridge, Mass.: Ballinger, 1986).
9. Paul Gray, "Competitiveness: A National Priority," *MIT Report*, March 1987, p.3.
10. Peter Bridenbaugh, Remarks at ASEE/ERC Forum, Washington, D.C., 2 March 1987.

2 INNOVATIVE INDUSTRY-UNIVERSITY LINKAGES: IS THERE A MISSING LINK IN OUR ECONOMIC DEVELOPMENT CHAIN?

Alvin L. Kwiram

Economic competitiveness has become a prominent topic in the 1980s, propelling an enormous range of activities in "economic development."[1] A number of bills that seek to create a more effective environment for economic development and technology transfer have been introduced in Congress. However, in contrast to many issues that temporarily grip the attention of policymakers in Washington, D.C., this one will be with us for a long time. The issue is not whether economic competitiveness is important, but rather, how it will be achieved.

In what follows, we will examine how an idea generated in the course of scientific research eventually becomes a product in the marketplace. While recognizing that this is a complex, multistep process, the present discussion will focus on its fundamental stages. I will argue that the traditional two-stage model is inadequate, and I will devote the bulk of this chapter to conceptualizing a third "linkage" stage.

Anticipating the later discussion, I will refer to three major stages. Stage I is the research stage, which, in its basic form, is carried out primarily in the research universities in this country. Stage II is the linkage stage. Stage III is the commercialization stage. We will consider each of these, but with the major emphasis on Stage II.

I wish to acknowledge the helpful discussions with Dr. Eric Dahl of the University of Washington.

17

The basic research enterprise in this nation's universities is the envy of the world. There is no doubt that in this stage (Stage I) we continue to be preeminent, because of both the quality and the quantity of such research. There are improvements that should and must be made, but one can argue that American universities are doing a very good job of basic research and today, at least, stand at the head of the class.

At the other end of the process spectrum stands the commercialization stage (Stage III), represented by the industrial sector of this nation. Until the last decade or two, U.S. industrial might was virtually unchallenged in the world. That situation has changed dramatically in the last decade. Nevertheless, despite intense competition from Japan, West Germany, and even emerging industrial powers, the U.S. industrial base is still powerful and is in the process of transforming itself to be even more competitive. Although important adjustments will have to be made, the general hope is that — apart from sociopolitical issues — U.S. industry can continue to be competitive with industry worldwide.

These two components represent the minimum number of stages necessary in the idea-to-product process. However, the theme of this article is that our performance leaves much to be desired in the linkage *between* the basic research stage and the commercialization stage. We have begun to realize that this intervening stage (Stage II) is relatively underdeveloped. The present view that the two major stages — as depicted in Figure 2–1 — represent an adequate description of the process may be obscuring some fundamental flaws in our approach and, thereby, limiting the effectiveness of our so-called "technology transfer."

In the past, the connections that were formed between the results of basic research and the exploitation of those results for the creation of new products has by and large been a nearly random process. Whether or not a given idea was ultimately developed depended on where it was published, who saw it, whether it was consistent with a given company's mission, or whether some entrepreneur happened to become the product champion.

This approach to harvesting the results of our enormous investment in basic research can be likened to the hunter/forager activities of primitive man. The process of identifying new opportunities has depended far too much on serendipity, on a catch-as-catch-can approach. Instead, we have to learn to domesticate the research/

Figure 2–1.   Model I: Historical.

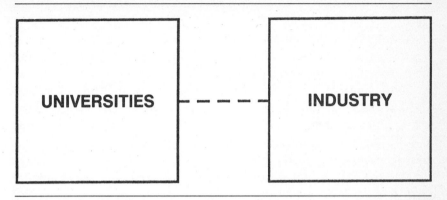

commercialization process, just as the more advanced societies in the past turned from foraging to farming so that they could domesticate livestock and control planting, cultivating, and harvesting in a systematic manner. We must do a much better job of capitalizing on the investment that this nation makes in the basic research enterprise.

We were able to tolerate the somewhat haphazard approach of the past in part because we had virtually no competition after the Second World War, but also because industry was faced with more opportunities to develop new products than it had time and resources to devote to them. Our earlier advantageous position has been dramatically altered. If we are to remain competitive, we must take a much more aggressive and systematic approach on this issue.

The problem of *linkage* has received too little attention in the past. We lack a clear understanding of the essential elements in the idea development process. Traditionally, the interaction between the basic research enterprise (based primarily in the university context) was linked only loosely to the industrial enterprise. The primary means of information transmission were:

- the students hired by industry, who brought with them ideas and skills learned in the university;
- publications (and patents) produced by universities, which were monitored by industry for their particular needs;
- consultants who served industry in their areas of specialization; and

- industry support of faculty for targeted research to address a recognized need.

That is the model represented in Figure 2–1. For at least ten years, these means of transmission have been recognized as inadequate, and many serious discussions have followed, aimed at finding a better way of increasing the linkage between the source of the new ideas and those who utilize those ideas to create new products or to improve the efficiency of production. Considerable effort has been directed toward the goal of bringing universities and industry closer together — to enhance university-industry interaction.

The new level of interaction can be illustrated by a revised model (see Figure 2–2), which represents the paradigm for a variety of industry-university programs that have been initiated in recent years.[2] This effort has been remarkable in the degree to which *attitudes* about industry-university interaction have changed in both camps. Nevertheless, there is less consensus about the degree to which the effectiveness of technology transfer has been increased, leaving aside the larger question of whether we are anywhere near the optimum in that process. Despite such concerns, the model represented in Figure 2–2 has tended to dominate much of the thinking behind recent efforts to improve industry-university interaction. It is worth mentioning a few examples of what has been achieved.

Some of the more notable efforts have involved entire industry groups that took the initiative to forge stronger ties with academe. For example, the Semiconductor Industry Association established the Semiconductor Research Cooperative to bring university investigators and companies together to focus on long-range research in semiconductor-based technologies. In 1979 representatives of the chemical industry launched the Council for Chemical Research (CCR). CCR includes most of the leading chemical and petroleum companies and virtually all of the Ph.D.-granting chemistry and chemical engineering departments in the nation. Numerous mechanisms have been developed by CCR to foster stronger interaction between industry and academe.

The federal government has also been active in this arena. For example, in the late seventies the National Science Foundation (NSF) introduced a program to establish industry-university cooperative research centers. This program requires industry participation in

Figure 2–2.   Organization Involvement in the Innovation Process.

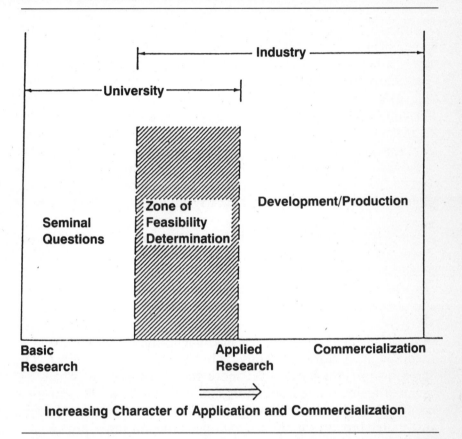

Source: National Commission on Research, *Industry and the Universities: Developing Cooperative Research Relationships in the National Interest* (Pasadena, Calif.: National Commission on Research, 1980), p. 5.

focused areas of university research. Over forty such centers have already been created.

One of the more successful of these NSF centers, the Center for Process Analytical Chemistry (CPAC), was established at the University of Washington. I will draw on our experience at this particular NSF center in order to examine the kinds of issues that arise in translating the results of basic research into the language of the world of technology.

In 1982 Professor Bruce R. Kowalski of the Department of Chemistry at the University of Washington proposed a fundamentally important concept that addressed a basic problem common to many industrial processes requiring chemical analysis at some stage of the production process. Whereas the automation of manufacturing has become increasingly sophisticated over the last hundred years (robotics being the most recent innovation), one of the critical elements has not been automated — the chemical analysis step. Even today, this function is most often performed at a central lab, where results of the analysis may not be provided for hours or even days, with the result that remedial adjustments of the production process are delayed. That approach is increasingly anachronistic. The solution to this long-standing problem is to incorporate the testing phase directly into the production line ("on-line") and to carry out the appropriate chemical analyses continuously.

This is a notable departure, in both concept and practice, for academe and for industry. In order to appreciate this, one has to understand the context in which this proposal was introduced. For several decades the discipline of analytical chemistry has been dedicated to the development of ever more sophisticated instrumental methods for the centralized analytical laboratory. This effort was supported by an array of companies that built the instruments used in the large central analytical laboratories of industry. But the increasing complexity of these instruments led to ever more costly installations, which demanded highly trained operators and carefully controlled environments. Clearly, such complex and costly instrumentation could not be distributed broadly for on-line, multipoint monitoring of processes in the demanding environment of a production plant.

By contrast, the new approach demands a major shift in emphasis. It requires the development of inexpensive, robust sensors that can be deployed in large numbers throughout the production facility. Powerful but relatively inexpensive microprocessors (personal computers or workstations) can then be linked to the sensors and, through the use of sophisticated mathematical methods (multivariate analysis), provide instantaneous and continuous analysis of the process. When combined with advanced control theory, the system can provide feedback to control the production variables, thereby automating this important remaining step in the production process.

That is the mission of CPAC, with its thirty-plus *Fortune 500* sponsors—companies like 3M, Dupont, Dow, Exxon, Hewlett-Packard, and Eastman Kodak. The goal is to monitor and control the entire manufacturing process, from the arrival of the raw material at the loading dock, throughout the entire production line itself—including quality control—to the characterization and disposal of the waste products. This approach need not be restricted to the petroleum refinery or the biotechnology plant. One should not have to wait several days for the results of one's blood tests at the physician's office. It is entirely feasible to develop on-line clinical testing instrumentation.

CPAC provides an excellent environment for industry-university interaction. It is unlikely that CPAC would have been formed in the absence of the NSF centers program. Now in its third year of operation, CPAC receives strong support from industry because this general approach to on-line process analysis and control of the production process promises significant bottom-line improvement for companies. (It is estimated that for a large company, losses due to inadequate quality can involve hundreds of millions of dollars a year.) But for the purpose of the present discussion, we need to ask how the results of the basic research that is being done by CPAC scientists are being adapted by industry for its own needs.

The NSF centers represent one of the more promising mechanisms for transferring technology from the university to the industry sponsors. One might expect that ideas would be adopted quickly by the appropriate sponsors and then developed. That is not necessarily the case. What actually does happen to new NSF center ideas and invention disclosures? A specific example from CPAC may serve to illustrate part of the problem and may suggest that even this exemplar of industry-university interaction does not seem to encompass all of the elements necessary to optimize the full range of technology transfer steps.

The octane rating that is posted on the neighborhood gas pump is obtained in a simple process. You start with an overdeveloped lawn mower motor worth about $150,000 and festooned with a variety of gauges and knobs. The technician injects about a pint of gasoline, and while the engine is running, the fuel mixture is adjusted until the engine begins to ping. The octane number is interpolated from standardized tables. The process takes about twenty minutes. That is how it is still done today.

It was known from earlier work that you could use near infrared spectroscopy to determine many important properties of fluid mixtures.[3] Normally, faculty members publish such results and go on to discover the next interesting phenomenon, without dedicating much time to evaluating the potential for commercial applications. In this particular case, following a conversation between two colleagues, Professors David E. Honigs and James B. Callis, it was decided to take the idea one step further because of the CPAC connection. Professor Callis obtained some standardized gasoline blends from one of the sponsors and, after the usual experimental refinements, demonstrated that you could measure the octane number (as well as half a dozen other important properties of gasoline) in about twenty seconds, using about 10 cubic centimeters of gasoline. Clearly, this represented a major step forward. No doubt sponsors would jump at the chance to get licensing rights to develop products for their production lines.

Actually, that has not happened. The petroleum companies would like to see someone develop a near infrared octane analyzer for them so that they can put it on their production lines, but they do not want to develop it themselves — they are not in the business of developing test instrumentation. Moreover, communication (technology transfer) between corporate divisions — Research, Engineering, Production, Quality Control, and so on — in a large company is often not as effective as one might like to think. The instrument companies will not initiate development because they do not see a sufficient market if they can only sell the devices to the petroleum companies. The entrepreneur is not jumping at the chance because the market possibilities have not yet been adequately demonstrated. Furthermore, the idea needs some additional prototype development. But who is going to do that? It is not the proper role for a faculty member. Indeed, the academic system is not designed to reward a faculty member who builds prototypes or who spends time worrying about patents and licensing.

The faculty member is no longer left entirely without help on the patent and licensing part of the problem. In 1981 the Bayh-Dole Act (P.L. 96–517) was passed. This law permitted the transfer to the university (as well as to small businesses) of intellectual property rights resulting from research carried out under federally funded grants and contracts. This new law stimulated a number of universities to establish something equivalent to an office of technology transfer. The purpose of such offices is to assist the faculty in developing their ideas for disclosure and patent applications as appropriate, to make contact with the business community in order to promote some of the research ideas, and to arrange for licensing, either directly or through other agencies.

This important support activity is now functioning in a purposeful manner at most major universities. But as the earlier example of the octane analyzer illustrated, good contacts with the business community may not be enough. What happens when there is a good idea, but there seems to be no one ready to step up to develop it?

One response is that there is a ready and eager venture capital community organized to step in at precisely this stage. There are indeed spectacular examples of highly successful companies launched by venture capital firms. In most cases, however, the major funds tend not to be interested in ventures that promise sales significantly less than roughly $100 million per year (order of magnitude). Moreover, in order to minimize risk, they are inclined to focus on projects already quite far along on the development path. Although the seed capital community is willing to step in earlier in the development phase, the restrictions on minimum projected market size tend to be similar.

Maybe the octane analyzer and other ideas that could be mentioned will find sponsors for the commercialization phase. However, many ideas are never developed, in part because they cannot generate the volume of sales necessary to make it feasible for a major company or venture capital enterprise to pursue. But how many $100 million companies do we initiate in a year? Maybe one can generate a comparable level of economic activity and employment with ten $10 million companies, as recent studies have suggested.[4] West Germany has learned this lesson well. Just last year they became number one in total exports worldwide.[5] And they are doing it with hundreds of smaller companies, together with their BASFs and Bayers and Siemens and Hoechsts.

The question we have to ask is whether the mechanisms that exist today for commercialization are adequate to systematically harvest the fruits of our research investment. What about the roughly 95 percent of the ideas that are rejected by the venture and seed capital community? What about the many ideas with a potential of only $10–20 million in annual sales? Although there are smaller (usually private placement) funds available in such cases, the principals may be less able to put together an appropriate business plan or a management team, much less to foster and promote further targeted R&D. What about the near infrared spectroscopy idea that might never have been applied to the octane problem if the NSF-sponsored industry connection through CPAC had not existed? How many other ideas are being generated but not developed for want of either a technology pull or science push? Do we have an adequate infrastructure in place *at the critical stages of the process* to systematically nurture and capture a significant fraction of the research output of our universities? Maybe by relying solely on the private sector we force the decision point for commercializing an idea or technology too far to the low-risk end of the spectrum. Maybe we need to experiment with new structures that would allow that decision point to be shifted so as to include some higher risk ventures. It has been argued that the ease of technology transfer is inversely related to the degree of novelty of a new technology.[6] Incremental changes in technology are generally the most readily accepted by industry. Thus, the more profoundly innovative the new technology or idea, the more it may have to be developed before it will be found attractive to the business community.

There are plenty of anecdotal examples of the faculty member who has had a good idea (maybe even a blockbuster, though not on the then current list of the hottest top ten topics), but who has not been able to find anyone interested in pursuing the possibilities presented. In rare cases, such a faculty member with sufficiently strong convictions, a low risk-aversion quotient, and the fortitude of an explorer might decide to become the product champion. His or her options are limited. It normally means leaving the academic position, borrowing money from friends, and trying to develop the concept or device. That approach is usually counterproductive. The universities do not want to lose their creative faculty members, but the faculty member cannot retain his or her position while fully engaged in commercializing a product. Ideally, such a faculty member should be able to remain at the university and at the same time serve as a resource person and consultant for a group of seasoned professionals who take responsibility for further development of the idea to determine feasibility and to develop a prototype.

To reiterate, many ideas that spill out of the basic research laboratories are still too embryonic for the commercial (Stage III) environment. They need more nurturing before an entrepreneur (industry) is willing to take the risk and assume responsibility for the project. The university, on the other hand, is not designed for developmental activities, and it would be a distortion of its mission to serve that purpose. Moreover, the incentive structure in academe is inappropriate. The reward system focuses on publications and the peer recognition that results from introducing new ideas. Further, the training of students at the graduate level requires an emphasis on the creation of new knowledge, not the refinement of what is already known, or worse, the building of prototypes.

Thus, even promising ideas can become orphans — rejected by academe as no longer novel or worthy of further attention, but not adopted by industry because of uncertainty about their viability, about possible hidden defects, about their true potential for long-term health and vitality. Academe, though it has conceived the idea and delivered it in more developed form after a period of gestation, often lets the product of its labors suffer the consequences of inattention.

This suggests the need for an environment where these embryonic ideas for potential products can be nurtured and brought to a stage at which they are more attractive to industry. In other words, the issue is not that of a simple one-step *transfer* of technology from academe to industry. Indeed, there will in general be several technology transfer steps involved. At the very least, there may need to be a transfer of concepts between the basic research phase and an applied research phase — and then later, one between the applied phase and the product development phase. Alternatively, one could say that the task is to translate the ideas generated in the research environment so that they are in a form more acceptable, or in a language more recognizable, to industry as potential winners.

The thrust of the above arguments is that even the model represented in Figure 2–2, for which CPAC is an excellent exemplar, may be inadequate and must be supplemented by additional structures, such as those represented in Figure 2–3. The circles can be thought of as representative of various spheres of activity (literally and figuratively). Thus "industry" represents small companies, venture capitalists, large companies and any other entities directly engaged in developing a product for the marketplace. The university sphere represents any of the basic research entities, including national labs, not-for-profit labs, and so on. If one views the circles as representing spheres in three dimensions, then one can imagine other spheres (entities) linking the university sphere with the industry sphere and overlapping with each other.

In other words, one can think of the linkage pathways in terms of substantial "parallelism." In the simplest version of this third model, we could consider a single linking sphere between industry and academe that is designed to translate the results of basic research into the language of the commercial sector. We will refer to this sphere of activity as the linkage sphere. The corresponding institutional structures would be so-called "technology institutes," or just "institutes" for short.

Figure 2–3.   Proposed Model.

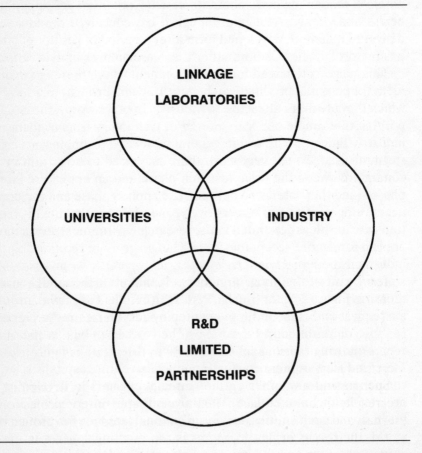

How would such institutes, or science-to-technology transfer laboratories, be supported? The essential elements would include the following four major components.

1. Substantial federal funding.   At the present time the federal government supports roughly 90 percent of the basic research costs at universities. By contrast, in many cases industry supports virtually all the costs of commercialization. In view of the discussion above, the institutes would require a support structure somewhere between the two extremes.

2. Significant funding support by industry on some matching basis.
The primary purpose for involving industry is to keep the process focused on practical goals, and to bring industry's experience to bear. In other words, the expertise of industry is essential to help define market issues, to advise on how a development might be optimally directed, and to suggest what evolutionary form would be of greatest interest to industry. Individual companies could choose to support specific projects of interest. Alternatively, this support could take the form of a consortium similar in some ways to the NSF centers for industry-university cooperative research.

3. Each institute must be associated with at least one research university, and must be situated in close proximity for maximum interaction.   The institute can be administered by the university, but not simply as a standard division of the university. As indicated earlier, the incentive structure for the professional staff must be different from that characteristic of normal university appointments. A structure more like that of the national labs, or a modification thereof, seems more appropriate.

4. State government must contribute to the support of the institute.   All states are interested in economic development and must take an increasingly aggressive approach in the future, not unlike the attitude that characterizes the individual states in West Germany. By supporting such ventures, states can help spread the cost while at the same time improving the chances that efforts in their territory may lead to increased local economic activity.

Such institutes would have another major advantage. In contrast to the results of basic research that are reported in the professional journals and are instantly available to all interested parties around the world, the results of developments in the institutes would naturally and appropriately have much more restricted visibility. This would provide a way of differentially capitalizing on our substantial investment in basic research. By linking companies to the early stages of development in an environment (the institute) that is a hybrid between the complete openness of a university and the protected environment of industry, our industries would have a significant time advantage for exploiting the results of the work carried out in the institutes. In a more global sense, such institutional structures could also reduce the conflict between the academic community and federal policy regarding proposed restrictions on the flow of scholarly information across national boundaries.

Such an institute could encompass a number of secondary features that would make it the focal point for economic development in the state and would help to facilitate the commercialization process at the local level. For example, an office of technology transfer could be closely affiliated with the institute. Likewise, an incubator could be associated with the institute to help enterprising entrepreneurs launch new ventures. The state and various economic development councils and agencies could locate appropriate offices for economic development and trade there. The university, through its regular and extension programs, could mount short courses, conferences, and regular seminar programs on a wide range of topics involving new business opportunities, entrepreneurship, and the latest ideas coming out of the research labs. The institute would serve as a meeting place for business interests, the university, government, and other interested agencies. In short, the institute could serve as a focal point for economic development in the region.

Equally important, by assuming responsibility for these economically oriented activities, the institute would provide an important interface between the university and the business world, while at the same time serving as a buffer to reduce the chances that commercially oriented activities would distort the fundamental mission of the university.

Superficially, it might appear that the NSF centers already incorporate many of the institutional characteristics outlined above. There are several reasons why the centers as presently designed are not the appropriate vehicles to carry the primary burden of technology transfer to industry. Not only is the level of NSF funding inadequate to start with, but it decreases to zero within the five-year period of the grant.

It remains to be seen how many of the present centers will be viable in the long term, once federal funding has ended.

But more important by far is the intrinsically different character of the work carried out in the centers compared with that of the institutes. The centers engage in basic research that is oriented toward problems of interest to industry. The work of the institutes emphasizes development and begins roughly where that of the centers ends. (Clearly, the boundaries between all of these elements are rather ill-defined, but for the sake of brevity we restrict ourselves to these general terms.) The culture needed for the intermediate development stage (Stage II), which lies between the basic research phase and the commercialization phase, is different from that of the university and that of industry. It is most like that of the national laboratories.

There are those, of course, who argue that the federal government should stay out of the development arena and leave such efforts to private enterprise. Many economists argue that such a hands-off policy is inappropriate for *basic* research. If one accepts that view, it simply shifts the debate to the task of identifying where on the continuum from research to development, government support should be reduced to zero (and how abruptly—with respect to the continuum axis, not the time axis).

Others suggest that no further structure or government support is needed because the best ideas will ultimately emerge and be successfully developed through private investment. They would argue that if an entrepreneur does not see adequate potential in an idea or if private funds cannot be attracted to a project, it probably does not deserve to be supported. In other words, the present array of barriers along the development path represents an essential mechanism for weeding out bad ideas. This argument is a commercial version of the evolutionary dogma of "the survival of the fittest." It can be most easily disposed of by taking it to its logical extreme, namely, that the way to ensure that only the very best ideas ever see the light of day is to make the development and commercialization process as difficult as possible. Increased government regulations, lack of venture capital, disadvantageous tax, trade, and antitrust laws, increased cost of capital, and other barriers should be designed and placed in the development path. The "survival" position seems absurd when stated in that form. On the other hand, it would be equally absurd to squander resources to support ventures that have no prospect of success. But surely one can imagine a broad range of projects in between that could benefit by support and encouragement in the early stages (given fairly rigorous timelines for meeting specified goals). The question is whether the present system for nurturing and exploiting the results of basic research is optimum. Generally, one tries to reduce barriers that stand in the way of achieving potential goals. Can we afford to do less in the high-technology economic arena?

There is no doubt that the marketplace will ultimately judge whether an investment (by private enterprise, or with government support) was prudent or not. On the one hand, if the government provides too much hand-holding, one runs the risk of wasting resources in support of something that will not survive in the open marketplace. On the other hand, there is always the need to maintain a balance between the full subsidy of basic research and the full industry funding for commercialization. But we must not expect only successes. Unless we have a certain number of failures, we are probably not exploiting enough of the ideas that are candidates for the marketplace. We have to find the proper balance point as we enter the increasingly competitive economic environment of the twenty-first century.

The concepts outlined above are not entirely unrelated to a challenge faced by this nation in the nineteenth century. In the 1860s the nation felt a strong need to enhance the development of agriculture and engineering. A farsighted Congress enacted the Morrill Act, which established the land-grant colleges. The impact of those institutions, and especially of the agriculture colleges and later their extension programs, has been enormous. Part of this success, especially in agriculture, was, of course, due to the well-defined and limited nature of the problem — providing better equipment, seed, fertilizer, and pesticides for a standard array of crops.

The challenge today is no longer predominantly in the natural resources sector. The challenge today is in high technology — in manufacturing and industrial development. Maybe what is needed today is a Morrill Act for the twenty-first century — a national economic development (extension) program associated with our research universities. Such a program would need to be established with a clear understanding of the problems that need to be addressed. It would require a different culture, a different incentive structure than either industry or the university provides. The NSF centers and various similar state programs can be thought of as steps in that direction, but as I have tried to illustrate, they may generate even more ideas to be exploited, thereby simply making the problem of harvesting the results even more serious.

There is little doubt that the university environment provides much of the intellectual raw material used in building the products of the marketplace. The more critical question is how much the raw materials need to be processed before industry finds them sufficiently attractive to single-handedly assume the risks associated with development. Although universities will increasingly have to play a leading role in supporting economic development and in ensuring that such activity is carried out in a systematic and optimum manner, they must do so without distorting the primary purpose of the university.

The nation has never been as challenged as it is today to handle the results of our enormous investment in basic research in a systematic manner. We have simply assumed that good outcomes would follow automatically. Our task is to find the requisite structures and processes whereby our society can be effective in achieving maximum productivity from its investment. This will be necessary, though not sufficient, to remain economically competitive. We can no longer afford the luxury of relying on serendipity.

NOTES

1. See, for example, Peter Drucker, *Innovation and Entrepreneurship: Practice and Principles* (New York: Harper and Row, 1985); National Science Board, *Industry-University Research Relationships: Myths, Realities and Potentials*, Fourteenth Annual Report of the National Science Board (Washington, D.C.: U.S. Government Printing Office, 1982); IC² Institute (University of Texas, Austin) and the RGK Foundation, *Technology Venturing: Making and Securing the Future* (Austin, Texas: 1985) and *Commercializing Technology Resources for Competitive Advantage* (Austin, Texas: 1987); "Industry/University Cooperative Programs," Proceedings of a workshop held in conjunction with the 20th Annual Meeting of the Council of Graduate Schools in the United States, Las Vegas, Nevada, 2 December 1980 (sponsored by the Council of Graduate Schools and NSF); Business Roundtable on International Competitiveness, "American Excellence in a World Economy," 15 June 1987; National Governors' Association, Center on Policy Research, "Making America Work: Jobs, Growth, and Competitiveness," July 1987; and Lester C. Thurow, *The Zero Sum Solution: Building a World Class American Economy* (New York: Simon and Schuster, 1985).

2. Examples include Pennsylvania's Ben Franklin Partnership Program, Ohio's Thomas Alva Edison Partnership, the Washington Technology Center (at a more modest level of state support), and many others.
3. David E. Honigs, T. B. Hirschfeld, and G. M. Hieftje, "Near Infrared Determination of Some Physical Properties of Hydrocarbons," *Analytical Chemistry* 57 (February 1985): 443.
4. David L. Birch, "The Job Generation Process," MIT Program on Neighborhood and Regional Change, (Cambridge, Mass.: MIT, 1983).
5. Timothy F. O'Boyle, "Sales Success: German Firms Stress Top Quality, Niches To Keep Exports High," *Wall Street Journal*, 10 December 1987 p. 1.
6. D. B. Illman, J. B. Callis, and B. R. Kowalski, private communication and *American Laboratory* 19, no. 12 (December 1987): 6–8.

II | ENTREPRENEURIAL MANAGEMENT IN BIOTECHNOLOGY

3 BRINGING SCIENCE TO THE MARKETPLACE

Herbert W. Boyer

I would like to begin by making a confession. I am not a businessman, although in my high school yearbook I declared that my goal was to be a successful businessman. Between my high school graduation and the beginning of my first year of college, I changed my major from accounting to biology and chemistry. These were the subjects I enjoyed the most.

I firmly believe that success requires dedication, a consuming interest, and enjoyment in one's chosen career. This should be obvious, but many young people will choose a career for other reasons. They might make significant contributions, but unless the intellectual commitment and drive have enjoyment as a companion, success will be difficult. I think it might be appropriate to briefly narrate my scientific career to help set the scene for my discussion of the founding of Genentech and the transfer of science from academia to industry. This will be a personal view of how technology that I was intimately involved with was transferred to Genentech.

SCIENTIFIC EDUCATION

As an undergraduate at St. Vincent College in western Pennsylvania, a small liberal arts school operated by the Benedictine order, I first learned of the discovery of the structure of deoxyribonucleic acid, better known as DNA. This discovery of the structure of the genetic material is one of the major milestones in the history of the biological sciences and ranks with the discoveries of Newton, Einstein, Darwin, and other giants of science. I became quite interested in genetics as an undergraduate, and the Watson-Crick discovery provided the spark for my decision to go on to graduate school and do research in the developing science of molecular genetics.

At the time I entered graduate school at the University of Pittsburgh (1958), molecular genetics was in a truly primitive stage. For example, the genetic code, the basics of which were provided by the structure of DNA, was estimated by eminent scientists at the time to be solvable in twenty years (which would have been by 1980). It actually was accomplished in 1961.

Research for my thesis dissertation could be facetiously categorized as the study of "sexual dysfunctions in bacteria." Then and even today this might generate derision and cynicism in some circles, but in fact this research eventually provided the keystone for recombinant-DNA technology and for the founding of Genentech. When I was a graduate student the most popular organism for molecular genetic research was bacteria. My research led to the discovery that the fertility of sexual matings between unrelated bacteria was controlled by a set of closely linked genes. I was so taken by the theoretical nature of these genes, and by the way their products could affect DNA at a molecular level, that it provided the basis for my scientific career.

Properly motivated, after finishing my Ph.D. I was off to Yale University for a three-year postdoctoral fellowship and what my wife hoped was the end of my school years. At Yale I continued my research on the nature of these genes that affected sex in bacteria, while at the same time learning all I could about protein and nucleic acid biochemistry. I have an enormous gratitude for my education at Yale, largely because I developed into an independent scientific investigator over those three years.

In 1966 I came to the University of California at San Francisco as an assistant professor and with the goal of determining the nature of the gene products (or proteins) responsible for the intriguing effects on DNA. At UCSF I had a small laboratory, a research associate, a few graduate students, and modest support from the National Institutes of Health, the National Science Foundation, and UCSF. After some frustrating research failures, we were able to purify one of the products of the genes responsible for the sexual problem in mating bacteria. In 1969 we were able to show that this gene product, now known as a restriction endonuclease, is capable of recognizing DNA of an unrelated organism and of cutting it into fragments. The basis for sexual dysfunction in mating bacteria was explained. The female bacterium, as a result of possessing the restriction endonuclease, could recognize DNA donated from unrelated male bacterium and destroy it by cutting it into pieces. This restriction endonuclease, which we named "EcoRI," was used for the first recombinant-DNA experiment.

The EcoRI endonuclease turned out to have a property that prompted us to initiate the first recombinant-DNA experiments. This property was the way in which it cut DNA—namely, it generated fragments of DNA with "sticky" or "cohesive" ends. Since the enzyme recognized a sequence of six base pairs in DNA, the sticky ends made at these sequences are identical and could be rejoined in a covalent or permanent fashion. Thus, fragments derived from any DNA molecule by the EcoRI endonuclease could be permanently rejoined, or recombined, with any other fragment of DNA generated by the EcoRI endonuclease, regardless of its origin.

The first recombinant-DNA experiment was done in collaboration with Professor Stanley Cohen's laboratory at Stanford University. This involved cutting the DNA of a South African frog (Xenopus laevus) with the EcoRI endonuclease and recombining it with a small DNA molecule taken from the bacterium E. coli, which also had been cleaved by the EcoRI endonuclease. All of these procedures were done in a test tube. The next step was to insert the recombined DNA molecule into a bacterium, a process known as "bacterial transformation." Because the piece of bacterial DNA to which the frog DNA was permanently attached was a miniature chromosome, it would be replicated in the transformed bacterial cell and passed onto each successive offspring. We demonstrated that transformed cells that had received the DNA molecule could be recovered at a practicable frequency and that the DNA molecule, or cloned DNA, could be obtained in large quantities for additional studies and modifications.

This experiment became the basis for the first patent to be awarded in the recombinant-DNA field. While today all scientists in the field are sensitive to the value of patents, in 1973, when this experiment was done, we were quite naive about patents. (Many scientists at that time thought that government-supported research could not be patented.)

Stan Cohen and I never even thought about a patent for our invention. As a result of considerable attention from the media, the Patent and Licensing Office at Stanford realized that our invention should be patented. After our initial misconceptions about patents were corrected, we went on to work with the patent offices at Stanford and the University of California. Eventually, on 28 August 1984, we were awarded U.S. patent no. 4,468,464 for "biologically functional molecular chimeras." Patent no. 4,468,464 is now the most lucrative patent held by the University of California. Genentech today holds and has applied for several hundred patents.

By 1974 it was clear that recombinant-DNA technology would have a profound effect on the biological and biomedical sciences. Indeed, today virtually every laboratory in these fields uses the technology in one way or another. However, at the time of the initial DNA experiments it was not at all clear that it would be feasible to transfer the technology to industry for the generation and manufacturing of new and useful products. Coemerging with the recombinant-DNA technology were two other technologies that had synergistic effects on each other and provided the foundations for biotechnology as we know it today, and for the founding of Genentech. These technologies were the chemical synthesis of DNA from basic chemicals that could be obtained from bottles on the laboratory shelves. This made it possible to adapt and modify DNA molecules cloned from any natural source, to synthesize genes, and to provide useful chemicals to aid in the cloning of rare DNA molecules. The third emerging technology was the determination of the sequence of the basic chemical elements of DNA that specify the genetic code. Thus, it became possible to determine the complete genetic code of any fragment of DNA isolated by the recombinant-DNA technology.

By 1976 my laboratory at UCSF had integrated all three of these technologies into our experiments. One of the key experiments on the pathway to the founding of Genentech was a collaboration with Drs. Arthur Riggs and Keichi Itakura at the City of Hope Medical Center in Duarte, California. We were able to recombine a small piece of chemically synthesized DNA (simply recreated from a known bacterial gene) with one of the small bacterial chromosomes, transform it into bacteria, and show that it could replicate and function. Soon thereafter I received a telephone call from Robert Swanson.

IS RECOMBINANT-DNA TECHNOLOGY READY TO BE TAKEN TO THE MARKETPLACE?

That is the question that Bob posed after a peremptory introduction. Without hesitation, I replied in the affirmative. We arranged for a brief meeting late the following Friday afternoon. Our initial discussions were cordial, and I was taken by the idea that Bob was thinking of starting a new company based on recombinant-DNA technology. At five or so, we decided to go for a few beers at a fern bar on Clement Street to explore the idea further. For the next several hours we outlined our strategy. We formed a partnership, put together a business plan, and established our immediate goals. Within a few months we incorporated Genentech, Inc.; that was in 1977.

Bob has an undergraduate degree in chemistry from MIT, but as he said, "without a green thumb." He then received an M.B.A. from the Sloan Business School and eventually found his way to San Francisco as a junior partner in the venture capital firm of Kleiner and Perkins. His goal was to start his own company after learning the venture capital field. Having been impressed with what he had read about the burgeoning recombinant-DNA field, he thought this might provide the beginning of a new industry.

One of our first goals in 1977 was to demonstrate that the recombinant-DNA technology could be used to make a product. Our first proposal was to synthesize a gene for human insulin, insert it into a bacterium, and have the bacterium manufacture insulin for the treatment of diabetes mellitis. After additional consideration, we thought it would be more expedient to substitute a gene (for a human brain hormone, namely, sommatostatin) for the human insulin gene. With this plan in hand, we obtained our initial funding from Kleiner and Perkins and arranged to have the research carried out under contracts to my laboratory at UCSF and the laboratories of Drs. Riggs and Itakura at the City of Hope. By the end of the summer of 1977, we demonstrated for the first time that recombinant-DNA technology could be employed to genetically engineer a microorganism that would manufacture a human brain hormone. This provided us with the armament to approach the venture capitalists for the substantial funding required to put Genentech on the map. We had a good story.

CREATING AN EXCITING ENVIRONMENT

Bob and I agreed that we needed to attract the brightest young scientists we could find in order to take the new technologies from the university laboratories to the laboratories at Genentech. This would be the first step in transferring the recombinant-DNA technology to industry. We provided salaries better than those of most universities, facilities, stock to reward their sharing of the risk, and the freedom to publish their research in scientific journals. This last commitment has the drawback of informing our competitors of what we are doing, but it is important for the development of the reputation of scientists within Genentech, and perhaps more importantly it commands the respect of scientists outside of industry. This leads to collaboration and channels of communication with the entire research community. In a way this brought about a spirit of excellence and competitiveness at Genentech that has spread throughout the company.

In our newly acquired and modest facility at South San Francisco, our handful of bright young scientists set off to engineer a microorganism that would produce our first product, and the first product of the biotechnology industry. Within the first year we had a bacterium that would synthesize human insulin. At that stage of Genentech's evolution we took the option of licensing our first product to Eli Lilly Company, for manufacturing and marketing. Given the status of Genentech at that time compared to that of Lilly, the world's dominant supplier of porcine insulin, we felt we could not continue to develop products and at the same time compete with Lilly.

However, Bob was adamant that we become a "fully integrated company," and we set out to hire a complete management team, using the same approach we used to attract scientists. We wanted the best young management team that we could find. Before we had a product to market, we had a vice president of manufacturing and a vice president of marketing. Naturally we have a cadre of bright young lawyers—corporate, patent, and so on. Bob's dictum from the day we first met was: "In order to be a successful company we not only must develop products, we must manufacture and market them."

Our second product, which we developed, manufactured, and took through the FDA approval process, was human growth hormone. The first year of sales of human growth hormone has produced sales of nearly $44 million—one of the more successful first years of sales for a new product on record. Our sales force is as enthusiastic and competitive as our scientific force.

GENENTECH TODAY

Genentech is a pharmaceutical company with a leadership position both in developing DNA products and in bringing to market products based on this technology. In 1986 Genentech had total revenues of nearly $134 million, over 1,200 employees, and facilities of 837,000 square feet, including 160,000 square feet of manufacturing space. We have FDA approval for a major pharmaceutical product, tissue plasminogen activator, which we market as Activase. This is a natural product of the body, and we manufacture it in mammalian cell culture; it attaches to and dissolves blood clots and is used by physicians to treat heart attacks and other clotting disorders. These products and others will propel Genentech into the ranks of the world's leading pharmaceutical companies. Our scientific efforts are now divided into three areas that define our product interests: molecular immunology, cardiovascular biology, and developmental biology. These research areas utilize the recombinant-DNA technologies on a routine daily basis.

REFLECTIONS

The successful transfer of recombinant-DNA technology from academia to industry occurred in a way that might not be applicable to other technologies that will emerge in the future. However, several lessons might be learned from this example.

If fate, or "karma," had never put Bob Swanson and myself in San Francisco in 1976, with our separate but convergent career goals, I believe that this particular technology would have eventually been picked up by the established pharmaceutical companies, such as Lilly and Merck. In fact, they have done so in the past few years and now represent our most serious competitors. However, I also believe that it would have taken much longer without the creation of Genentech. The established companies in 1976 were not staffed with scientists engaged in the emerging recombinant-DNA technologies and did not have the vision and faith to take the risk of incorporating this field into their research and development efforts. The success of Genentech provided the impetus for the established companies to get on the bandwagon and led to the creation of numerous other start-up companies as well.

It was important to attract to Genentech young creative scientists actually conversant with and competent in the field. It was important to create an exciting and stimulating environment for our scientists if they were to discover and develop new products. It was important to attract young and experienced creative management personnel if we were to have all the components for a successful manufacturing and marketing company. It is important to maintain this creative environment and to nurture it so that new ideas and discoveries are made by Genentech scientists; in addition, such an environment enables us to recognize important new developments emerging from academia.

Today our knowledge base in the biomedical sciences is so powerful that we anticipate an ever increasing understanding of disease processes, as well as of normal biological processes. It is important to maintain an environment that preserves the best of academia while concentrating on the goal of developing new products. Collaborations between business and academic scientists can accelerate the discovery process and provide revenue to the academic institutions.

Naivete is one factor that might be overlooked by someone who has not actually experienced the transfer of technology to industry. I believe that Bob and I had no idea that it would take so much effort and funding to get our first product to the marketplace and to identify and develop new products. Chance, necessity, enthusiasm, and naivete all contribute to the successful transfer of technology to industry. They are the intangible elements that made Genentech successful.

4 BRINGING BIOTECHNOLOGY TO THE MARKETPLACE

Kathleen M. Wiltsey

Bringing biotechnology products to the marketplace has stimulated the creation of new business practices as well as new industries. Several pharmaceutical products produced by biotechnology have been developed, as shown in Figure 4–1. Five of these biopharmaceuticals products have already been approved by the U.S. Food and Drug Administration: insulin, alpha interferon, human growth hormone, hepatitis B vaccine, and tissue plasminogen activator. One of the products well along in human testing is Amgen's recombinant erythropoietin, the protein that stimulates red blood cell production. We will use Amgen and its recombinant erythropoietin product, EPOGEN™, to illustrate how management practices have evolved in the entrepreneurial biotechnology industry.

ENTREPRENEURIAL MANAGEMENT

The classic activities involved in developing and commercializing a new technology are shown in Figure 4–2. The overall mission and goals of the company drive the unifying strategy for each functional activity within the company. For example, Amgen's mission at the time of its founding in 1980 was to build a major, fully integrated pharmaceutical business based on advances in recombinant DNA and molecular biology.

45

Figure 4–1.   Therapeutic Agents Produced Through Biotechnology.

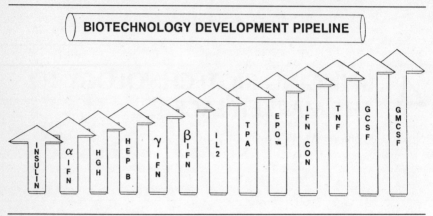

Figure 4–2.   Managing the Development of a New Technology.

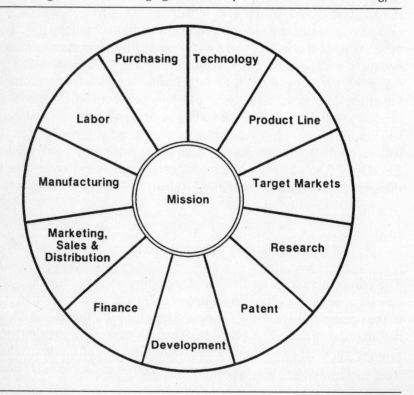

TECHNOLOGY, PRODUCT LINE, AND TARGET MARKETS

From this core technology of synthetic and recombinant-DNA technology, the company has developed products in four business areas: human pharmaceuticals, human diagnostics, animal health care, and specialty chemicals. Human pharmaceuticals remains the area of greatest emphasis, and the goal is still to develop products, from cloning through to direct selling. Amgen was the first to isolate and clone the human erythropoietin gene, and produce recombinant erythropoietin. EPOGEN™ is likely to be Amgen's first product to the market, sold by its own sales force. In addition to EPOGEN™, Amgen has five other recombinant products in human trials: granulocyte colony stimulating factor (G-CSF), interleukin 2 (IL-2), gamma interferon (IFN-γ), consenus interferon (IFN-Con), and hepatitis B vaccine.

RESEARCH AND DEVELOPMENT

A cell's DNA controls the production of its proteins, as shown in Figure 4–3. If you can obtain minute quantities of a desired protein-Dor its corresponding messenger RNA — from a natural source, scientists may synthesize a gene to produce that protein. Alternatively, the gene itself may be isolated from a natural source. Scientists then can insert this gene into a productive cell type to produce the desired protein in large quantities and at high purity.

Figure 4–4 shows the subsequent product development steps for pharmaceutical use. The safety and efficacy of the therapeutic agent is first assessed in animal studies. If the therapeutic agent exhibits beneficial biological activity and an acceptable safety profile, it may proceed into human clinical studies. Once safe and effective use has been demonstrated within the target patient population, the company seeks the approval of the regulatory agencies to market the product. The manufacturing process is scaled up to ensure commercial supplies, and when the FDA approves the product, marketing begins.

Let's consider the research and development of recombinant erythropoietin as an example. Erythropoietin is a protein that is normally produced by the kidney and circulates through the blood stream to the bone marrow where it stimulates precurser cells to mature into red blood cells. The kidney secretes erythropoietin in response to reduced

Figure 4–3.   Protein Synthesis.

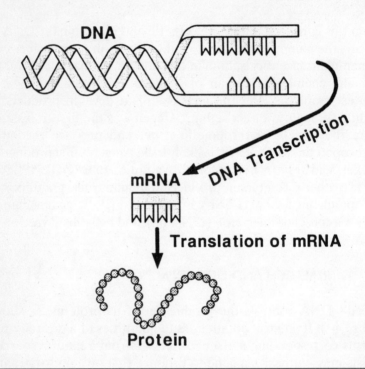

oxygen tension in the tissues. As more red blood cells are produced, more oxygen is carried to the tissues by hemoglobin. This cycle is illustrated in Figure 4–5.

Patients with impaired kidney function, such as patients with chronic renal failure on dialysis, do not produce sufficient quantities of erythropoietin and, as a result, develop chronic anemia. Many become extremely fatigued, unable to work or continue their normal activities. This is the initial target population for recombinant erythropoietin therapy.

While the existence of the hormone erythropoietin has been known since 1906, the protein is produced in such minute quantities that it could not be purified for therapeutic use as human growth hormone and insulin have been. Obtaining the human erythropoietin gene was an extremely difficult endeavor with no guarantee of success. A very persistent scientist, Dr. Fu Kuen Lin of Amgen, devised a clever way of isolating the human gene based a new method of screening human

Figure 4–4. The Development of EPOGEN™.

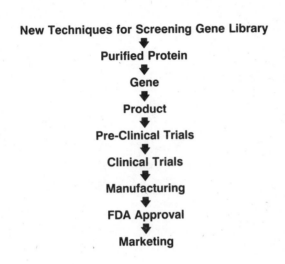

New Techniques for Screening Gene Library
↓
Purified Protein
↓
Gene
↓
Product
↓
Pre-Clinical Trials
↓
Clinical Trials
↓
Manufacturing
↓
FDA Approval
↓
Marketing

genomic libraries. After two years of long days and nights in the laboratory, Dr. Lin had the human gene! He was the first to succeed, and his success placed Amgen in the leadership position worldwide in developing this therapeutic agent.

Amgen's EPOGEN™ product since has been shown in clinical trials to elevate the red blood cell level of dialysis patients, relieving their anemia. The primary way to increase dialysis patients' red blood cell levels has been by transfusion, and many of them require several transfusions a month. Transfusions expose patients to a very small risk of hepatitis B and AIDS infection, but numerous transfusions can also cause serious iron overload and can immunologically sensitize a patient, sometimes increasing the risk of kidney rejection in the event of a transplant. The elimination of transfusions among dialysis patients would be a major medical advance.

The elevation in red blood cell level (*hematocrit*) and the elimination of transfusions in dialysis patients treated with Amgen's EPOGEN™ can be seen in Figure 4–6.

The results of the first human clinical trials were published in the January 8, 1987 issue of the *New England Journal of Medicine* and the

Figure 4–5.   Formation of Red Blood Cells.

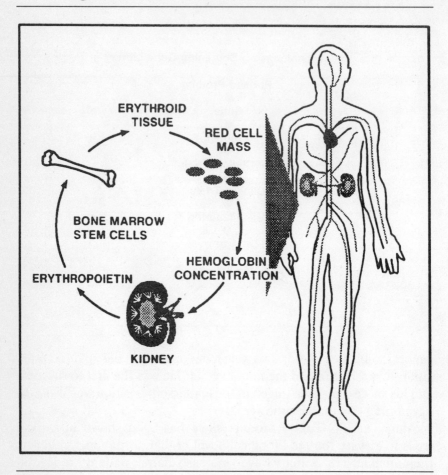

November 22, 1986 issue of the *Lancet*. Following these publications, *Business Week* published a favorable article entitled "The Hormone That's Making Amgen Grow."

Amgen has filed patents around the world on its recombinant erythropoietin technology to protects its leadership position.

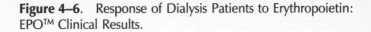

Figure 4–6. Response of Dialysis Patients to Erythropoietin: EPO™ Clinical Results.

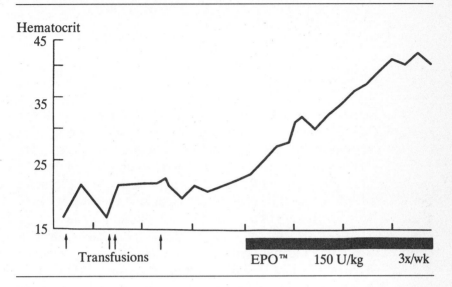

FINANCE, MARKETING, AND SALES

Clinical trials are very expensive, and biotechnology companies must seek significant financing to pursue clinical testing.

There are numerous options for a start-up company to finance product development: private equity placement, public stock offering, R&D limited partnership, debt, licensing technology to a corporate partner for development, or licensing partial rights to a corporate partner and retaining rights to those applications you can commercialize yourself.

Amgen has used private and public equity offerings, corporate partnerships, and an R&D Limited Partnership to fund its research. For EPOGEN™, the company retained marketing rights to the dialysis market in the United States, and licensed rights to other applications to Kirin and Johnson & Johnson. By this strategy, Amgen is able to realize its goal of becoming a fully integrated company while collaborating with well-financed partners to commercialize additional opportunities around the world.

In addition to a share of the profits downstream, Amgen also receives milestone payments now for specific development achievements, which account for most of the company's revenues at this point.

MANUFACTURING

In manufacturing, Amgen scientists have employed their synthetic DNA technology to achieve very high yields in a variety of production systems, including mammalian cells, yeast cells, and *E. coli* cells. Amgen scientists will try all three optimized systems and will choose the most efficient one for production of each product. In the case of recombinant erythropoietin, a particular mammalian cell was selected as the production system. The human erythropoietin gene was inserted into this cell, which produces recombinant human erythropoietin. These cells become minifactories, and colonies of cells are grown which produce large quantities of recombinant erythropoietin, which then is isolated and purified. A state of the art commercial manufacturing facility has been built to produce commercial quantities of EPOGEN™.

PEOPLE

Attracting and retaining skilled people is a crucial factor in a start-up company. Many of the biotechnology companies have attracted research scientists from academia and top executives from major corporations by offering them greater challenge and discretion, as well as part ownership in the company. Every employee at Amgen receives stock options and is part of the team. These factors contribute to a high level of motivation and commitment among employees.

A wide range of skills is required to bring a biotechnology product to the marketplace, as shown in Figure 4–7.

PURCHASING

Biotechnology is not as asset-intensive — and purchasing is not as critical a function — as in many industries. In fact, people say that, in biotechnology companies, the assets walk out the door at the end of the day!

Nonetheless, it is interesting to note that a related industry has emerged — suppliers to the biotechnology industry. Companies that supply the instruments to synthesize genes and proteins, the specialized manufacturing equipment and supplies, and even software for genetic engineering, reached profitability before their biotechnology customers.

Figure 4–7. Skills Necessary for Biotechnology Commercialization.

THE CAST

Scientist ➡ **Molecular Biologists**   ➡ Sales Rep
+   **Protein Chemists**   +
Gene   **Gene Synthesis Chemists**   Product

Assay Development Scientists
Pharmacologists
Immunologists
Process Engineers
Manufacturing
Quality Assurance Scientists
Clinicians
Regulatory
Finance
Business Development
Marketing

BIOTECHNOLOGY MEANS NEW PRODUCTS

The biotechnology industry has created opportunities for new medical therapies, based upon the body's own biochemical processes. Already we have seen five human therapeutics enter the U.S. market, and the probability of success for numerous others is judged to be high. Through the understanding of molecular biology, it is now possible to work *with* nature in preventing and fighting disease.

5 THE BIOTECHNOLOGY INDUSTRY AT THE CROSSROAD

G. Steven Burrill

The biotechnology industry stands at a crossroad. It is making the transition from the laboratory into the marketplace — emerging from the research and development phases with marketable products. According to the U.S. Department of Commerce, by the year 2000 the biotechnology market could be worth $40–100 billion. Biotech products represent enormous potential for bringing profit to our economy and better health care to millions of people. However, as they mature, biotech companies must prepare to enter new financial phases, meet new crises in management, and resolve new strategic issues. Some of the most important issues facing biotech companies today include regulatory concerns, foreign competition, the question of whether or not to integrate vertically, and financing tactics.

CRITICAL ISSUES

Regulation

The regulatory process is somewhat in flux, with unclear requirements and processes. Industry leaders have pointed out that government support, through legislation, is needed to shield some of the industry's key products from liability suits. On the other hand, will government supervision and federal regulation become so protective that they delay the progress to be made in marketing viable products? And what about state and local regulations? Who will be answering the regulatory questions—scientists knowledgeable about the products, businesses that understand their economic potential, lawyers building legal precedents, or activists using alarm tactics?

Patents

New product innovation is expensive, in both time and capital, so patent protection becomes crucially important to companies that hope to secure a profit from their investment. Yet, few legal precedents exist for determining what constitutes patentable items. As new products and methods emerge from labs all over the country, law suits over patent issues proliferate. These suits are costing the industry significant dollars as companies spend potential research funds defending their rights to the results of that research. Litigation also takes away the time biotech companies could be spending on more productive endeavors. Until precedents are established, the need to finance court battles may make it prohibitively expensive for a young company to enter the biotech market.

Foreign Competition

The U.S. biotechnology industry also faces challenges from abroad. Although generally slower than U.S. firms to enter the biotech race, Japanese and European firms now promise to become strong, well-financed competitors. In Japan particularly, large firms have a history of changing the balance of power. The potential progress of such giant firms cannot be ignored. If U.S. biotechnology companies hesitate, perhaps because of regulatory restrictions or financing needs, they will be overtaken. In the constant search for capital, the U.S. biotech industry may sell itself out, winning the race in the short term but losing in the long term.

Vertical Integration

To become a vertically integrated company—to achieve self-sufficiency and to finance R&D expenses through operating revenues—seems to be the ultimate goal of most small biotech enterprises. But is this goal realistically worth pursuing? In fact, industry analysts expect only a few companies to become fully integrated. A company planning vertical integration must finance the costs of gearing up manufacturing facilities and marketing forces. It must make a choice about which of the products currently in development it can afford to market. The company must be clear about the commercial niches that its product will occupy, its ability to dominate those niches, and whether or not the products can be used easily by customers. As it begins to sell products, the company will also have to balance the money spent on research and development against the money spent for manufacturing and sales. Management will likely notice a shift away from revenues from interest on R&D contracts and equity deals toward increased revenues from sales.

SUCCESS FACTORS

Certain key elements typically figure into the overall success of a biotech company: building a strong management group, meeting the needs of the marketplace, developing truly innovative technology, and bringing appropriate financial resources to the enterprise in a timely fashion.

The Management Factor

Most agree that good management is the most important factor in any company's success. However, the concept of management works differently in a biotech company because many biotech companies were conceived and founded by researchers, scientists, even Nobel Prize winners—individuals who are gifted in scientific matters, but often not well trained as managers. The real task for the management of a biotech company is to take the science and convert it into something profitable. This means that the career paths between the technologist and management must be separate and distinct.

The Marketplace Factor

The technology of the product is ultimately useful only from the standpoint of meeting a market need. Too many biotech company executives believe that the "product sells itself" and fail to take into account the importance of actively marketing their product. Therefore, it's vitally important to understand marketplace dynamics, competition, and distribution channels. Smart management understands the "unfair advantage," or distinctive competence, their product has over the competition. Positioning the product in the marketplace is important because the buyer takes more into consideration than just the technical quality. Timing is also essential. The product may be introduced too early — before the public is ready to accept it. Or the introduction may be too late — the competition is already entrenched and thriving on a large market share. Successful biotech companies understand the dynamics of the window of opportunity, position their products for the right time and place, and then stay in touch with the market. The key is not so much to develop innovative technology, but to solve real customer problems and concerns.

The Technology Factor

Surprisingly, the technology itself is not the most important factor in the "successful biotech company equation." What makes new technology valuable really has little to do with its patent or copyright, albeit those are important. The most important element is its built-in "barrier to entry," or uniqueness — a quality that is so intrinsic to the product or technology that it would be difficult or impossible for someone else to replicate the technology in a timely or cost-effective manner. For example, in the pharmaceutical therapeutics business, the barrier to entry is higher than in diagnostic product development.

The Financing Factor

Will there be sufficient funding available to continue building this industry? As a practical matter, only a few financing options can be considered. What is really at issue is management's ability to assess the company's stage for growth and match it with the optimal financing choice for that stage. In addition, management must be aware of changing trends in the investment marketplace, which fluctuates in response to a variety of economic conditions. By matching the company's growth stage with available financing opportunities, management can inventory adequate amounts of capital for future growth cycles.

Venture Capital and Private Financing. Venture capital and other sources of private funding have been the financial mainstay of biotech start-ups. Is the market too crowded to warrant financing start-ups? A broad-based biotech company that seeks to finance science activities in the hopes of stumbling upon a viable product is not likely to attract capital. Investors today are more willing to finance a narrowly focused, market-driven opportunity. This is true not only for venture investors, but also for businesses forming alliances with small companies.

Because they foster a creative and open atmosphere in which scientists feel at home, small companies can be very efficient shops for the development of new products. They have a unique and vital role to play in the industry as incubators of new ideas and technologies. Many industry experts think the cures to major diseases are most likely to emerge from such companies. That is why it is so important for venture capitalists and other kinds of private investors to continue to make funds available to start-up and early-stage enterprises. If the biotech company is working on a specific product, and if the product appears to be nearing the market, its business plan is likely to attract investors. As in virtually all industries, the first few companies to market a product usually achieve and retain dominance in that niche. The management of small biotech companies must be certain they are bringing new concepts to an investor. A new generation of biotech start-ups is being born now.

Going Public. The public equity market can be a major source of financing for a biotech company, but at the expense of dilution. Solving big problems — such as finding the cure for cancer or AIDS — is an alluring prospect for the American investor. The crusade is appealing from a humanitarian perspective, but it is also attractive because early investment in a company that solves such a big problem will generate large rewards.

The initial public offering market is cyclical and fluctuates. To determine which stocks are most likely to increase in value, investors cannot rely on traditional financial indicators. The industry is still too young to have generated those numbers, and so would-be investors must track the development of each company's technology. Which cancer cure is progressing most quickly and appears to be closest to the market? Which companies have the potential to become major manufacturers? When a company goes public, its valuation usually depends on the promise of its products or the credibility of its contracts with other corporations. What are the actual strategic costs of going public? Understanding not just the financing opportunity but the strategic implications—this is a critical success factor.

Strategic Linkages.   As they mature beyond the start-up stages, many companies seek financing through joint ventures. While these joint ventures take various forms, they are basically strategic alliances between smaller biotech companies and larger pharmaceutical, energy, chemical, and agricultural companies that have existing manufacturing and marketing operations. In the earliest stages, these joint ventures frequently necessitate some compromise. Although the larger company often assumes the risks associated with developing products that may not work, the smaller biotech company frequently surrenders 40–70 percent gross margins to realize only 5–10 percent royalties. Nevertheless, the arrangement has several advantages for the young company. Although it doesn't realize a huge return on product sales, the smaller company builds credibility for its products, receives the larger company's help in getting FDA approval, and can take advantage of established marketing resources to commercialize its product. In fact, joint ventures may provide a reliable method for financing successful biotech companies that decide against becoming fully integrated entities. And for larger companies it provides a unique access to new technologies and products, at very reasonable costs.

Acquisitions.   The prospect of profits from a successfully marketed product has encouraged many major firms to acquire biotech companies. A much publicized example is Eli Lilly's acquisition of Hybritech.

Is this really the direction of the industry? If so, what are the implications? How do you keep innovation alive in a formal corporation structure? For the biotech industry, innovation is embodied by key research personnel, and this underlies the importance of retaining key employees.

Debt Financing.   Traditional debt financing is rarely done by young biotech companies. Companies that have a long product development time and intensive R&D expenditures cannot be relied on to adequately service the debt principal and interest. Secondly, biotech companies — especially in the start-up phases — represent a risk factor that is too high for traditional lenders. If a financing deal is put together with debt, it's usually in the form of convertibles. The deal can be arranged to give maximum flexibility to the company, so that the debt comes due only when the company should be most able to pay it.

What is really key about all these financing options is understanding the market conditions — and therefore the probability of the financing happening — and the effects of the financing on strategy.

CONCLUSION

The biotechnology industry has reached a series of crossroads. New companies have passed the "take-off" stage and have brought successful products to the marketplace. Science of the purest and most basic form has been converted into products. But many business choices lie ahead. Will biotech start-ups enter long-term joint ventures with large pharmaceutical, agricultural, and chemical companies in marketing and manufacturing? When will full vertical integration be the strategy chosen? What combinations of the two strategies appear appropriate — both in the short term and the long term? When will it be wisest to be acquired by larger firms? If a biotechnology industry endures, what form will it take? These are the intriguing and adventuresome questions that entrepreneurial managers will face in the exciting years ahead.

III ENTREPRENEURIAL MANAGEMENT IN ADVANCED MATERIALS COMPANIES

6 ADVANCED MATERIALS SYSTEMS AS COMMERCIAL OPPORTUNITIES

John J. Gilman

This chapter will not tell you how to become rich and famous by commercializing advanced materials. What I will try to do is provide some perspective about trends in this field as they relate to future industrial opportunities.

One of the first points to be appreciated about materials is that, while the number of interesting substances in the world is vast, the number of commercial materials is relatively small. Sometimes newly discovered substances become developed into materials, but this is rare because a large number of constraints must be overcome before it can occur. The constraint that most often blocks commercialization is manufacturing cost, but there are many others, including safety features and the degree to which the profile of the physical properties of the new material matches the profiles required by specific applications. These profiles were quite simple many years ago, but they continually become more complex.

Historically, the properties of commercially used materials were determined by the primary producers.[1] This started at the mines and their associated smelters, at the clay pits and their potteries, at the forests and their lumber mills, and so on. Whatever they produced was what the user had to work with. As methods for fabrication became

Acknowledgment: This work was supported by the Director, Office of Energy Research, Office of Basic Energy Sciences, Materials Sciences Division of the U.S. Department of Energy, under contract no. DE–ACO3–76SF00098.

more advanced, the variety of shapes that could be manufactured increased, and the property profiles of products became increasingly determined by the methods used by fabricators to make semifinished mill products. Later, the emphasis shifted to finished products that were differentiated by the material they were constructed from. That is, there were discrete metal components, ceramic components, plastic components, and so on.

The culmination of this period is represented by the advent of components made of polymeric structural materials. Polymers can be formed into complex shapes inexpensively, so the market for polymeric objects developed rapidly, even though raw polymers are relatively expensive and do not possess outstanding properties. This is quite different from the growth of the steel industry earlier. The success of steel was based on inexpensive raw materials combined with outstanding engineering properties.

In the past several decades, integration has been occurring.[2] This has been shifting commercial opportunities to industries that use materials and away from those that produce them. It has also been increasing the demand for extensive profiles of properties, as contrasted with the relatively narrow profiles that were needed when materials formed clearly differentiated components of machines.

One consequence of the trend toward integration is that the functions of materials have become much more important than their places of origin or the costs of their raw materials. This trend will continue in the future because it is here that materials technology will make the greatest advances, and it is here that the greatest fractional utility is added. For example, a pound of aluminum as ingot is worth roughly $1.00. After conversion to a semi-finished structural shape, it is worth perhaps $5.00 per pound, but after conversion to a microconductor on a silicon chip, it is worth about $500 million per pound! Most of the value comes, of course, from the processing that integrates the aluminum into a system.

Another way to make this same point is to consider the elasticity of demand for materials. For commodity materials, price elasticity is high, so large changes in consumption cause only small changes in price.[3] But for materials that have been integrated into systems, price elasticity is relatively low, so small changes in consumption lead to substantial changes in price. Both cases only apply to "normal" — that is, competitive — markets. Since low elasticity helps to maintain gross margins, business operations in this arena will tend to prosper more than those dealing with commodities.

Still another indicator is relative price changes.[4] By this I mean price changes relative to an average change of zero for the economy as a whole. Some relative changes are increases, and some are decreases, while the sum of all relative changes is zero. For many years (at least twenty-five), the relative real prices of commodity materials have been decreasing. At the same time, the relative prices of materials in sophisticated integrated systems have been increasing. Thus, materials in their commodity forms have been getting relatively less important commercially, while the opposite is true for their integrated forms.

What I have said so far has been a preamble to saying that commercial opportunities in the materials area lie principally in materials systems, and much less in components made from differentiated individual materials. I'll try to clarify the difference through some examples.

The phrase, "material system," implies an operational function. Therefore, in considering where commercial opportunity lies, it is important to ask, "What functional areas are likely to grow most in the foreseeable future?"

Some of the technologies that are likely to show major growth in the future are:

- Photonics
- Robotics
- Prosthetics
- Astronautics
- Nanoelectronics

I shall discuss some of the materials systems associated with these technologies, with selected examples of the new materials that are involved.

PHOTONICS (OPTICS)

Electronics has been based on the large ratio of charge to mass for electrons, a ratio that allows them to be manipulated efficiently. The particles of photonics, namely photons, have neither charge nor mass.

Their lack of mass allows them to be manipulated at very high frequencies, making them useful in communication systems. They are useful for fabricating materials because their lack of charge allows them to be concentrated into very small volumes.

There are two principal branches of photonics. One is optical communications (including data processing) in which advanced materials are needed to generate, transmit, detect, analyze, focus, and display light. The other principal branch is materials processing, in which advanced materials are needed to make powerful lasers, as well as systems for manipulating and controlling the beams of light they emit.

For example, outstanding advances have been made in the purification of materials so that they can transmit light over long distances. In a few years this capability was improved by a factor of 10,000 compared with the best of previous glasses. (See Figure 6–1.) The performance of pure glasses in terms of transparency is truly spectacular. (See Figure 6–2.)

There is not enough space here to describe the many other new materials that are involved with photonics, but I do want to describe a relatively simple device that illustrates how various functional materials can be integrated to perform a higher level function.

Figure 6–1. Dramatic Reduction in the Absorption of Light in Glass in Recent Years.

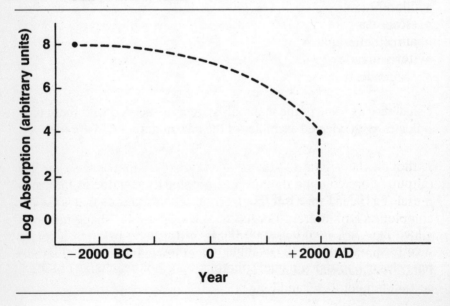

Figure 6–2.   Comparison of the Transmission of Light Through Two Forms of Glass.

Material	Transmission Distance (inches)
Window glass	0.2
Glass fiber	6×10^6

A battery-operated laser that emits a highly collimated beam of green light does this by means of the following chain of functional events: a battery provides electric current to drive a small array of gallium arsenide lasers, which emit light that excites an yttrium aluminum garnet rod, which contains fluorescent neodynium ions. This rod lases, emitting a beam of infrared light. The infrared beam then passes through a crystal of lithium niobate, which converts it into a beam of green light. Thus the device consists of an integrated series of materials, each of which performs a specific function.

ROBOTICS

Although the inputs to robots are critically important, so are the outputs. For actuating the outputs, nothing as versatile as biological muscle has been found thus far, but one actuator design that is close to completion is of interest. For its "muscles," it uses a "shape-memory" alloy. This is a metal that remembers its shape prior to a phase-transformation that is induced by temperature. In the case of a robot hand, the material there is actuating wires that are short above a certain temperature, and long below the same temperature.

These actuation wires are heated by electric currents to make the fingers bend and the wrist rotate. The result is a robotic system that is lighter and much more compact than those actuated by hydraulic cylinders or stepping motors.

PROSTHETICS

There is a powerful demand for improved prosthetic materials systems. It is generated by accidents, disease, violence, and aging of the population. Perhaps the most commonly known system in this class is contact lenses. Dental prostheses are also well known.

Most nonbiological materials irritate living tissues—some mildly, some severely enough to induce carcinomas. One of the most benign and therefore potentially most useful is pure carbon. The biologically benign aspect of carbon has been known for millennia by people with tattoos. A hard form of it, known as "glassy-carbon," has been used for many years in artificial heart valve systems. But a disadvantage of glassy carbon is that it is quite brittle; also, it is extremely stiff, which often makes it mechanically incompatible with biological tissues, including bone.

In recent years, considerable work has been done on the development of composites consisting of carbon fibers embedded in carbon matrices. These are called "carbon-carbon composites." They are mainly intended for high-temperature applications such as engines and rocket nosecones, but they have considerable potential for prosthetics. For certain levels of porosity, they can be both compliant and tough (nonbrittle). These properties, combined with their high level of biocompatibility, make these composites highly desirable for prostheses.

ASTRONAUTICS

Astronautics includes both the exploration and the exploitation of space. Both will require new power supplies, probably of the nuclear fusion variety. Implosions driven by ion-beams appear to have the best chance for success in realizing the necessary controlled fusion reactions. For building effective ion-acceleration systems, materials that can be quickly and easily magnetized are needed—among many others, of course.

The speed with which a material can be magnetized depends on the mobility of the magnetic domain-walls within it. As these move, they change the magnetization. A dramatic improvement in this property occurred in recent years with the advent of metallic glasses. These are made by cooling selected alloys very rapidly from the liquid state. As a result, there is too little time for them to crystallize, so they retain the glassy structure of the liquid.

Because of the ease with which metallic glasses can be magnetized and demagnetized, they have made it possible to build very efficient transformers that are being used in the distribution system for electric power. (See Figure 6–3.) Such transformers have the potential to save large amounts of energy each year (up to 35 billion kilowatt-hours per year).

In addition, these new materials have made it possible to design the huge magnetic switches that are one of the keys to the ion-accelerators needed for controlled thermonuclear reactors, which in turn are needed for advances in astronautics. Switches that weigh a few tons

Figure 6–3. Large Effect of Using Metallic Glasses for Transformer Cores on Loss of Electric Power.

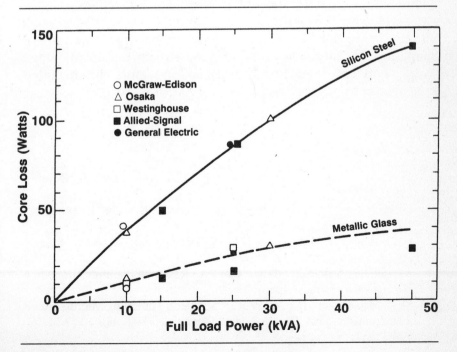

and can switch terawatt-sized pulses of electric power have been built from metallic glasses. The pulses consist of as much as one million amperes at 2.5 million volts.

NANOELECTRONICS

We are all familiar with the profound effects that microelectronic devices have had on our lives in recent decades. These devices have structural elements in them as small as one micrometer — that is, one millionth of a meter.

A new generation of even smaller devices is now being developed. They will be as small as one nanometer, or one billionth of a meter — which is the size of many individual molecules, and much smaller than many biological molecules.

Machining can also be done on a very fine scale.[5] This can be done through etching techniques that use ion-beams or photon beams, but it can also be done mechanically.

In closing, let me emphasize once more that the trend in advanced materials is toward integration. Materials and their functions are combined to form materials systems. These systems are fabricated by being built up "organically." This is occurring both on large scales, where composites are integrated into airframe structures, and on small scales, where semiconductors, metals, and insulators are integrated into nanoelectronic systems.

NOTES

1. G.L. Liedl, "The Science of Materials," *Scientific American* (October 1986): 127.
2. J.J. Gilman, "Material Processing: Opportunities and Challenges," *Journal of Metals* (February 1972): 51–54.
3. J.J. Gilman, "Demand Charts—Tools for Planning," *Research Management* (July-August 1987): 32–37.
4. J.J. Gilman "Price Trends as a Guide to Research Planning," *Research Management* (January 1980): 27–29.
5. M.A, McCord and R.F.W. Pease, "Scanning Tunneling Microscope as a Micromechanical Tool," *Applied Physics Letter* 50, no. 10 (9 March 1987): 569.

7 MANAGERIAL STRATEGIES FOR CREATING NEW MARKETS FROM NEW MATERIALS

Klaus Dahl

Raychem Corporation is a materials science–based company in the San Francisco Bay area that started with Paul Cook and a few others in a garage in Redwood City, California, in 1957. Now, thirty years later, annual sales are exceeding $1 billion.

Paul had the unique idea of putting radiation from nuclear waste products to some commercial use. This radiation primarily consists of alpha, beta, and gamma rays and is referred to as "ionizing radiation." Paul knew through his work at the Stanford Research Institute what kind of chemical changes ionizing radiation can cause in organic materials. Through prior experience and family connections, he also had significant experience in the manufacture of wire insulations. Therefore, he asked himself whether performance improvements would result from exposing ordinary wire insulations to ionizing radiation.

The use of a nuclear pile or a container filled with nuclear waste proved to be impractical, but a radiation source that could be turned on and off at will could provide a practical tool for experimentation and eventual manufacturing. The combination of controllable radiation, such as an electron beam, and the commercial knowledge of specialty wire manufacture thus provided the early technological foundation of Raychem Corporation.

The radiation of a semicrystalline polyolefin, such as polyethylene, primarily affects the amorphous regions of the polymer to create ions, free radicals, and their eventual recombination to form new bonds

73

that are called "crosslinks." When heating these crosslinked polymers above their crystalline melting points, the crystallites melt and the solid polymer is converted to a rubber. This rubber has enough physical strength to be useful for certain coating applications, for instance, wire and cable insulations. The rubber can also be stretched and then cooled to below its crystalline melting point. This cooling will convert rubber back to a tough resin while maintaining the new configuration. On heating the stretched piece of plastic, it will "remember" its original unstressed shape and shrink back to that geometry. This feature became the basis for a multitude of "shrink-to-fit" products.

Thus, from the beginning, the base technology of Raychem was one of creating unique materials, understanding their properties, and developing, manufacturing, marketing, and selling new products.

The first lesson for commercial success we learned was to depart from at least one position of strength (for example, the manufacture of specialty wires) by combining this strength with a synergistic new technology. Our strength was the detailed knowledge of how to modify organic polymers by electron beam radiation. In-depth intellectual involvement with this new technology and its quick application to generate new, albeit imperfect, products was the next step for creating what we call "lead customers."

Working with customers at their sites provided ideal "commercial laboratories" for testing the utility and desirability of the new products, which could be changed as needed to meet specific requirements. This method of operation avoided or minimized expensive and long-term investments in a new technology and product development without getting timely feedback. Another element of success was working with customers who had money for experimentation and were located close enough for frequent personal contacts.

Our initial customers were the aircraft and spacecraft industry in California and Washington State. They had an urgent need to reduce the weight of new jet aircraft that were designed to fly faster and farther. This design required materials of lower specific density to save weight and to provide improved heat resistance at higher operating temperatures. Our crosslinked, polyolefin-insulated wires provided a first answer. They were tougher, and therefore less polymer was required to provide the same insulation. They also displayed greatly increased heat deformation resistance — they would not melt when a wire overheated.

We developed multifunctional monomers as polymer additives to maximize the efficiency of radiation crosslinking. Other additives were selected from commercially available materials or synthesized to improve the oxidative stability and to reduce the flammability of the crosslinked polyolefin insulation for the range of intended service conditions. These efforts provided a strong proprietary basis and put us in a unique leadership position for the radiation processing of plastics.

Heat shrink products were developed to compete with electrical insulation tape initially. They proved to be easier to install and more reliable for insulating and for environmentally protecting electrical connections. Through upgrading of the base resin by additives, heat shrink products were created for more demanding environments, such as airborne vehicles, submarines, power stations, and sophisticated, high-density electronic equipment.

We then found that incorporation of conductive carbon into polyethylene and other polyolefins, followed by radiation crosslinking, led to electrically conductive polymers whose resistance would change by several orders of magnitude as the polymer was heated through its melting point. This phenomenon was reversible. Thus, we had the basis for a conductive polymer heater technology.

If one applies an electrical potential across a sheet of such a material, current will flow to generate heat internally until the polymer temperature exceeds the melting point of the crystallites of the polymer. Since the polymer is crosslinked, it will retain its shape and an adequate level of mechanical strength. The temperature of the polymer sheet will not exceed that of the resin's melting point, as the material's resistance is now too high to permit but a minor triggle current to flow. As a result, the polymer sheet thermostats itself to the temperature of the melting point of the chosen resin. These findings were then utilized to develop a multitude of heater and electronic control products.

CASE HISTORY OF A MAJOR RESIN SYNTHESIS DEVELOPMENT

The marketing and sale of our products to the aircraft and defense industry brought us in close contact with the future-oriented development and engineering organizations of these customers. This contact enabled us to learn about novel materials needs not yet met. Such a focus on real needs proved to be invaluable. It provided cost-effective research direction for new technology and product development.

The second generation, long-distance jets were designed to fly higher, faster, farther, and with much more payload. Aircraft weight and aircraft operating temperature became even more critical in design. Higher temperature meant 150–260° C for 10,000–50,000 hours of continuous operation. Virtually every additional pound of aircraft weight that did not go towards payload and fuel was scrutinized in great detail as to its necessity. In addition, safety requirements became much more stringent to minimize failure and allow for "safe crashes" in unavoidable accident situations. A shopping list of desired properties was compiled. The commercially available resins were screened. Reasonable modifications to be made to these polymers by their suppliers or by us were considered. But it became clear that no suitable resins existed to meet the new needs. In some ways, polyethylene or polyethylene terephthalate-Mylar type material came close, if satisfactory performance at 150° C and above could be assured. Principal concerns were mechanical strength, flame resistance, low smoke evolution in a fire situation, and resistance towards hydraulic fluids, gasoline, and other fluids encountered during ordinary aircraft operation. Since there was no match with commercially available materials, we embarked on a synthetic polymer program to create appropriate model compounds, to test them for performance, and then to devise practical polymerization schemes for the synthesis of resin quantities sufficient to prototype product evaluation. These investigations led to a new class of thermoplastic semicrystalline aromatic polymers — polyphenylene ether ketones — and to a pilot process for their manufacture.

The development work was completed in early 1970, and we provided wire and cable products to Boeing for their new 747 jumbo jets and to McDonnell Douglas for their DC-10 jets. Then the Arab oil embargo occurred. Both our principal customers reduced their plane production dramatically. As a consequence, we had to curtail and eventually shut down our polymerization operation. Unfortunately, at the same time we had not developed a sufficient number of alternate applications to support the resin output from our plant. The new resins displayed a broad spectrum of uses at temperatures in excess of 200° C, and they were nearly perfect for other electrical insulation applications. The process for their manufacture was a first in the industry, but it was costly in terms of overhead and capital. The sales volume of high-margin products needed to sustain the operation and improve upon them could not be realized, and we did not have the financial staying power to weather the temporary business slowdown.

In retrospect, we probably moved too fast, focused too hard on one product line, and undertook too ambitious a project for the size and financial strength of the company at the time.

However, we did not give up. First, we tried to sell the polymer technology as developed. Many of the people we approached liked the broad utility of the resins, but the manufacturing process was viewed as too hazardous and capital-intensive. We listened to the reservations voiced during all of the ensuing license negotiations, and through the persistence of a few scientists in our laboratory a much more practical manufacturing process was developed. We scaled it to the pilot level and then licensed the technology to a large European chemical firm. While all of this was going on, we managed to develop a small connector product line using the new resins. It was designed around the specific capabilities of this polymer class and focused on improving space utilization in aircraft. Our new connector product line now exceeds $25 million in annual sales.

Our polymer efforts did not go unnoticed. ICI, a large chemical company in England, developed and commercially introduced very similar resins in the late 1970s, using a different manufacturing technology and somewhat different resin compositions. Sometimes being a pioneer has its hazards, and one can never be too diligent and foresighted in patent drafting! More competition is on the horizon. In the 1990s we expect to see a number of additional manufacturers in the United States, Japan, and Europe. A broad range of uses for these new resins are now evolving for many engineering applications, including composites for vehicles for both ground and air/space transportation.

The lessons we learned from this effort are not all in yet. Some of us who started the effort may still be vindicated in our vision, but some obvious mistakes were made. One was not gathering all the available information at the time and entering into the venture as fully educated as possible. On the other hand, it is always easier to come up with more reasons for not starting something than for going ahead with it. Another lesson, however, became abundantly clear: there are some technology developments that are clearly very long-term in nature, and the developing of a new resin class clearly falls into this category. A company embarking on such an undertaking should be prepared to be patient for ten years or more before realizing major returns on its investment. Such a business approach also required the establishment of a strong and growing patent portfolio to protect the investment.

THE DO'S AND DON'TS OF INNOVATION

The guidelines for commercial innovations and their management vary from business to business. Some common denominators exist, particularly for the materials technology–based ventures. Peter F. Drucker summed up these guidelines in his recent book, *Innovation and Entrepreneurship*, and I would like to pass on his advice in the following paraphrase:

The Do's

1. Analyze the opportunities with a purpose in mind.
2. Conduct a conceptual and perceptual search. Keep it simple.
3. Start small. Try to do one specific thing.
4. Aim to be a leader — and stay there.

The Don'ts

1. Try not to be clever. Include morons as your customers.
2. Don't try to do too many things at once.
3. Don't try to innovate for the future. Innovate for the present.[1]

In addition to Drucker's rules, I would suggest some additional rules that we learned at Raychem over the years.

1. Take a known (to you) technology to a new market, or a new technology to a known (to you) market. Don't try to develop a new technology and a new market at the same time — it's very hazardous.
2. Always depart from at least one position of strength and offer a spectrum of performance improvements. One improvement alone seldom survives in the marketplace.

3. Ideas are cheap. Research and development are expensive. The major expenses, however, are incurred during scale-up, manufacturing, and market development. Therefore, do your homework extremely well before committing to a major project. Once started, it is hard to stop.
4. Once you have a good product line, go international but maintain a strong home market.
5. Become the best manufacturer of the product. Superior manufacturing assures a profitable life of a product line long after the patents have expired.
6. Research and development divorced from manufacturing, marketing, and selling tends to produce stillborn babies.
7. Use scientists/engineers with in-house sales training to market and sell products of high-technology content.
8. If you acquire a new technology, make certain it is complementary or synergistic with technologies you already use and control.
9. Develop technologies and products with lead customers. As they accept the products, other smaller or technically less sophisticated customers will follow.
10. Write performance specifications — these are another way of protecting your turf.
11. Price your product according to the market or functions served rather than on the basis of cost plus markup.
12. Watch the small guy who can run away with your business.
13. Never get fat, dumb, and complacent.

NOTES

1. Peter F. Drucker, *Innovation and Entrepreneurship: Practice and Principles* (New York: Harper and Row, 1985), pp. 134–137.

8 CREATIVE MANAGEMENT OF AN ADVANCED MATERIALS START-UP COMPANY

Ronald G. Rosemeier

Brimrose Corporation was started while I was a graduate student at the Johns Hopkins University in 1981. At that time, with a wife and three children and living on $600 a month, bringing money into the home was my main concern. In the fall of 1980, I had an opportunity to give a talk in England, where I presented some of my research work. After that talk, one of the scientists came up and asked where he could buy one of the X-ray instruments used in my research. That was the beginning of the Brimrose Corporation adventure.

The basic component of the X-ray instrument was developed by the military in the 1950s and 1960s. It was a night vision scope that allowed soldiers to see the enemy in the dark under starlight. My advisor at Johns Hopkins, Dr. Robert E. Green, Jr., had taken this component and modified it into a real-time, X-ray imaging device for use in the nondestructive X-ray testing of crystals and materials used in industry and the military. He developed the X-ray instrument ten years earlier and couldn't get it into the U.S. market. Curiously, I had to go to England to get it started.

When you start a high-tech research company, you have to address problems of start-up capital, cash flow, credit, and capital equipment. Where do you get the money to start? If you live in California, the conditioned response is to go to the venture capitalists. If you were born in Cokeburg, Pennsylvania, as the eldest son of a coal miner, you learn to be creative. When I first started, I had an order every two to three months for an X-ray imaging instrument, which I sold for $7,000. Can you imagine going to the bank with a pickup truck as collateral, with an income of $10,000 a year, and saying you'd like a loan for $4,000? The bankers laughed and said, "Come back when you have a credit history and are a bit stronger financially."

After numerous rejections from the banks, I saw a coupon in the newspaper with the advertisement headline, "$5,000 Line of Credit — No Collateral." I filled out the application and listed my position as "manager." (Never say "president" or "owner," because they want three years of tax returns, etc.) One week later I received a call for credit verification. I was the only one in my apartment answering the phone (while trying to keep the children from crying). The credit auditor asked to verify Rosemeier's income. I said, "Sure, hold on please." I pressed the "#" button on the phone to give the illusion of switching lines, deepened my voice, and said, "Hello, Accounting, can I help you?" "I'd like to verify Dr. Rosemeier's income," the auditor replied. "What did he put down?" I asked. "Sixty-five thousand dollars," she said. "I'm sorry, that's wrong," I said. "What?!" she exclaimed. "He makes $70,000," I replied. The next thing you know, within one week I received a book of checks from the credit card company stating, "You have a $5,000 line of credit."

Meanwhile, I paid the vendor $4,000 with a credit card check for the component item for the $7,000 order. After I got paid from my customer, I immediately paid off the entire invoice from the credit card company. Later, the credit card company increased my credit line from $5,000 to $6,000 for being such a good customer. Shortly thereafter, I started filling out more applications and obtained more credit cards. At the end of three years, I was able to raise $100,000 just by credit cards — no collateral. After establishing good credit with the credit card companies, I established "net 30–45 days" terms with our vendors, a provision that is critical to cash flow.

Another concern is equipment capitalization. In the beginning, I did a lot of "horse-trading" with universities. Among our biggest sources of new ideas and products are the universities. They have talented people doing state-of-the-art thinking. Professors have students on whom hundreds of thousands of dollars in research money has been spent. After the students leave, the professors generally never do this research work again. I always go to a university to find out what is going on and try to commercialize on that university's particular application. I have been very successful. The universities that I deal with on the East Coast are Johns Hopkins University, the University of Maryland, Rutgers University, and MIT.

One can hardly overstate the importance of getting the best people. Toward the end of the school year, I would go to all the top schools and ask for the two best students for an interview. I would select seven or eight of the best schools and pick out the top people.

I have a twenty-one-year-old woman running our entire administration, and she started when she was eighteen-years-old. She does an excellent job. Our policy is to try to bring in young people before they get corrupted. When I first started the company, I had a very hard time getting Americans who would want to take a risk with a company offering very low-paying jobs. I had no problem getting immigrants. My three top people were immigrants who had come to the United States with two garbage bags of clothes and old suitcases. These are people who left their countries, broke family ties, and came to this country with nothing. These are risk-takers. There are Americans like that also — of whom we have the best — but it is difficult to find them.

From the start of the X-ray Systems Division, Brimrose has expanded this market to include testing of gallium arsenide semiconductor wafers, which will be a future replacement for silicon. One of the problems with gallium arsenide is that there are very few techniques for nondestructive testing and evaluation of it before devices are made from it. If you look at it visually, after you polish it up nice and shiny, you would say it looks acceptable for making a device. But if you use a nondestructive X-ray testing technique, you can see that the crystal is not so uniform. However, some manufacturers build the device, then test it. And if the device doesn't work, they throw it away.

We've introduced some techniques by which we can look at these materials before and after devices are built with them. We're presently working with companies such as Westinghouse, Allied-Bendix, and Rockwell, as well as with the military, on developing a technique to look at gallium arsenide materials.

We've also taken variations of this technique and will be able to look at fibers such as dacron and nylon. The fiber companies can spin tons of material before they can test it and determine whether it's good. So it's very important to develop techniques that can quality-control these materials in real-time, using our X-ray imaging equipment.

We're looking at solid-fuel rocket propellants. They make tons and tons of these materials to put into the solid-fuel rocket motors, and the quality from point to point is not very good—they have many problems. We are also presently developing techniques further to be able to look at biological sensor materials.

People give us new materials and ask us to start investigating the commercial potential. So we asked ourselves, "Why not look in a particular niche of a market and ask whether we can start supplying some of the developmental semiconductors?" We picked a material that everyone is working on now, mercury cadmium telluride—a new infrared detector material that is going to be used in a lot of weapon systems. It is also being used on "Star Wars" systems, and the government has been spending millions of dollars for this particular material. We took a variation of this material that was developed in Eastern Europe and started reading the literature on it. We found that mercury manganese telluride is much easier to work with than the material they are spending all the millions of dollars on. And owing to the fact that it was a sister compound, the properties and techniques were similar. We used the millions of dollars of research to grow material and make infrared detectors. We also used our X-ray technique to quality-control good materials before we made devices from them. In this particular case, you can take one of those crystals, take a one-millimeter square out of it, and sell one of these infrared detectors for $7,000. If you keep processing a material, it keeps going up in value. So we were one of the first companies to introduce mercury manganese telluride infrared detectors. This was the beginning of our Infrared Division.

Using profits from the X-ray Division, we built an Acousto-Optics Division, which works on using sound to deflect laser beams. We are one of the few companies that was able to put vibrations in a crystal at one gigahertz. This translates into vibrating the crystal at one billion times a second, which causes the laser beam light to be deflected. Our competitor is a company in California called Crystal Tech, a division of Seimens of West Germany.

Again, we choose areas or markets that are very small but have a potential for a high profit and potential for high volume in the near future. We select techniques and put together systems that are very difficult for most companies to do. We always pursue challenging problems with solutions that create niche markets that are highly profitable.

Brimrose presently has twenty-five employees and has grown into a $3 million company. Our first sales and marketing vice president was hired to partially relieve our engineers from selling duties. We've established profit-sharing and a bonus program in our company. One of the keys to our successes has been finding people who work very hard and believe in what they're doing.

9 COMMERCIALIZING NEW MATERIALS: A 3M PERSPECTIVE

James A. Woolley

The 3M Corporation was founded on an "honest mistake." The founders of 3M entered business in 1902 to make and supply sandpaper. They thought they had purchased a site to mine a high grade of abrasive mineral on the shores of Lake Superior. The fact that no high-grade mineral existed there actually resulted in 3M's emphasis on quality, and quality assurance, from the very outset. Rather than close shop in the face of its false start, the company located another source of supply of the abrasive mineral and subsequently relaunched its business. The willingness to try, to risk failure in pursuit of success, and to "experiment in good faith" became the very root of 3M's culture. Furthermore, 3M engineers eventually found a use for that "fateful mountain of mineral in Duluth" when they launched 3M's fourth product line in 1932, roofing granules, which continues as a viable business today.

The early history of the company is closely tied to William L. McKnight. McKnight was hired as an assistant bookkeeper in 1907 and became a 3M legend in his own time. Rising through the ranks of the company, he came to hold the position of chairman of the board from 1949 to 1966. Those were years of steady growth and expansion of 3M's product lines, markets, and technology base. Underlying these results is the personal philosophy of business, values, and expectations that McKnight infused into 3M's culture. The most important of these are:

1. Belief in a strong free enterprise system
2. Vision of 3M as a growth company
3. The perspective of a global economy with the opportunity and need for participation in worldwide markets
4. The strategy of profit reinvestment for growth through self-financing
5. The expectation and goal of product diversification
6. The belief in the worth of pioneering research
7. The tactic of seeking patents to enhance the likelihood of getting an acceptable return on the results of pioneering research
8. The belief in competing on value, not on price
9. The policy of never blaming a person for an error resulting from honest effort
10. The practice of giving each employee the freedom to do a job in his or her own way
11. The policies of promoting from within and of keeping employees informed
12. The practice of taking care of innovators

These tenets are the basis for 3M's growth from a start-up based on a mistake to a $9 plus billion multinational, multimarket, multitechnology company. They continue to be the essential foundations of its culture.

ATTRIBUTES OF 3M'S CULTURE

Two key attributes of 3M's corporate culture are our continuing commitment to new business development and innovation and our demanding, yet nurturing and supportive, management team. These are illustrated by excerpts from the operating objectives of 3M's current CEO, Allen F. Jacobson: "To encourage and develop programs and management attitudes which will produce constructive innovation, appropriate risk assumption, and opportunity realization in all business functions . . . and to . . . develop the human resources necessary to meet business objectives."

The next six attributes of 3M's culture are really management strategies for achieving our primary goal of building new businesses.

Definitive new product targets challenge each business unit to have 25 percent of its sales in any given year from products less than five-years-old.

Business unit autonomy provides each division vice president with broad operating latitude to achieve the corporate financial objectives for which he or she is accountable. Within both the marketing and R&D communities, there is corporatewide emphasis on maximizing the commercialization of our existing technologies (which currently number about 100) while at the same time working relentlessly to create new technology. This is underscored by our corporate policy of technology-sharing. Management of markets and products is the responsibility of business units. But technology is a corporate resource, available to anyone in the company who needs it. This is a fundamental strength of 3M.

The "15 percent rule" allows any employee who has a product idea to spend 15 percent of his or her time pursuing it. While not everyone uses this "guaranteed" discretionary time, it is a powerful support for innovation and personal initiative.

To prevent good technical people from going into management positions just to "get ahead," 3M has a dual technical/management ladder system that recognizes and compensates research excellence and contributions on an equal basis with corresponding management positions.

Other attributes of 3M's culture reinforce a climate for innovation and its commercialization. "Patient urgency" implies that what one is doing is important and couples this recognition with the patience to persevere in the absence of short-term results.

Respect for individuals and their ideas is critical to creating and maintaining an innovative and entrepreneurial climate. Indeed, this was the very cornerstone of McKnight's management value system.

Celebration of successes has proven to be essential in reinforcing and sustaining the innovative process. This includes a wide range of recognition programs in all functions, plus such corporate recognition programs as "New Business Venture" team awards as well as "Circle of Technical Excellence" individual and team awards.

Just as important as celebrating successes is a constructive attitude toward failure. The company does not enjoy failure and does not encourage it. But 3M does encourage "experimentation." It views negative experimental results as constructive progress along the path to finding out what really works in the laboratory, in manufacturing, and in the marketplace.

The last attribute of 3M's culture is the company's *open and pervasive communication systems*. Management executives visit operations all over the world on a regular basis to keep in touch with the scope and spirit of what is going on. They also use these visits to show their own interests and to keep people informed. In addition, 3M has management councils for each major function and many cross-functional activities, like our technical forum that sponsors dozens of special-interest chapters and symposia to stimulate information exchange at the grass-roots level.

TECHNOLOGY ACCEPTANCE FACTORS

Technology acceptance requires that a technology satisfy real and immediate business needs. For this to happen, there must be customers who both have those needs and want them satisfied. In addition to this, anthropological research and the research of Dr. James Bright, the father of technology forecasting, have shown that there are eight factors (taken from the *user's* perspective) that are strong determinants of technology acceptance:[1]

1. Perceived advantage: The user must be able to easily see advantage in innovation to be motivated to embrace it.
2. Compatibility: The more compatible the user perceives a new idea to be with what he is already doing, the greater the likelihood of acceptance.
3. Simplicity: The simpler an innovation is perceived to be, and the lower the level and complexity of supporting activity required to practice an innovation, the less the resistance that will be encountered.
4. Divisibility: The more an innovation can be tried one piece at a time, the easier it will be to accept.
5. Communicability: If one can use "old" vocabulary to describe the "new" idea, it makes it easier to accept.
6. Reversibility: The more easily a user can withdraw an innovation without significant pain or cost, the more likely that an innovation will be evaluated.

7. Relative costliness: This is another way of saying "relative value" to the user. The relative cost of an innovation, including the degree to which it absorbs the user's time, money, people, emotion, and commitment, must be less than that of what it is replacing.

8. Failure consequences: The user must fully understand the consequences and probability of failure of an innovation. The lower the probability and seriousness of a failure, the more interested a user will be.

ENABLING FACTORS

In addition to these eight external factors for technology acceptance, there are three critical internal factors, which I call "enabling factors," that seem to be important to the innovative process, at least at 3M. They are:

1. access to customer needs and an understanding of those needs;
2. access to technology, with some insight into how the technology can be used to meet customer needs; and
3. the willingness to experiment.

Given this perspective as background, 3M's general approach to commercializing new materials is illustrated by the following model extracted from the works of Dr. Ralph Katz.[2]

Using its knowledge of customer needs gleaned from its involvement in multiple markets, 3M generates market-driven product concepts. It uses its researchers' knowledge of technology, based on access to multiple technologies, to generate technology-driven product concepts. Through a process of collaborative screening and experimentation, the company distills probable winners for development and market testing.

While 3M may not do this perfectly, the company's experience is consistent with research results that emphasize the importance of a strong technical-marketing partnership and a project portfolio that consists of both market- and technology-driven ideas.

If the results of research on innovation are correct — and innovation really is a random process that occurs in the least likely place, at the least likely time, and is accomplished by the least likely people — then 3M's approach is to try to create its own microcosm of the world by encouraging lots of people to try lots of things in the hope of capturing an above-average share of unpredictable events.

NEW TECHNOLOGY IN AN OLD MARKET

Two examples will demonstrate how this happens at 3M. The first deals with introducing a new technology in an old and established market and turning the industry upside-down by setting a new standard for performance.

When I first joined 3M in 1971, I entered the corporate research laboratories, which at that time had the responsibility for both pioneering research and technology-building. Soon after, I met Dr. Hal Sowman, who was investigating the synthesis of novel ceramic materials from very pure inorganic salts. Since he had already been working in this area for three to five years, he had demonstrated — and was in the process of patenting — novel compositions and product forms like fibers, flakes, and beads and was actively looking for market applications in which his innovation could be used. One such product/application was novel high-temperature ceramic fibers for making high-temperature composites.

This eventually became 3M's Nextel-brand ceramic-fiber product line, which has been used to make the insulating-tile heat shields on the space shuttles. But this is not the reason for the story.

Dr. Sowman and a colleague in 3M's Abrasive Product Division, the home of 3M's original "sandpaper" business, had started to collaborate on the possibility of making superior abrasive grains. This was fortunate because after more than seventy years of relying on fusion furnaces to make abrasive grain, one of our competitors, Norton Company, introduced a new mineral that represented a significant improvement, and 3M needed to respond. That was in 1972. A joint research team was quickly formed, but it took four years of effort to demonstrate that, indeed, superior minerals could be made using Dr. Sowman's approach. Having made this breakthrough, there was only one problem — the cost of the raw materials was exorbitant and uneconomical compared to that of the traditional fusion process.

In the face of the threat of loss in market share, 3M researchers persisted until, two years later, changes in chemistry and processing resulted in achieving both performance and economic feasibility. Pilot quantities of the new grain were made and test-marketed in 1979, and a production-scale operation capable of producing tons of material per day was commissioned in 1982.

These minerals are marketed under the brand names of Regal and Regalite. After more than ten years of effort to respond to a competitive threat, 3M turned the industry upside-down because of a materials breakthrough that has set new industry performance standards and opened the way, through continued research, to make even further improvements. This case history clearly demonstrates the main thesis of 3M's approach: A clear understanding of market needs, access to technology to meet those needs, the willingness to experiment, and perseverance — with patient urgency — are key enabling factors for commercial success.

MULTIPLE APPLICATIONS AND MARKETS

The second example illustrates 3M's success at exploiting a given technology in many applications and markets. The technology in this case is nonwoven webs. In 1942, 3Mer Alvin Boese discovered that plasticized cellulose acetate fibers could be run through hot calender rolls and fused into a unified, clothlike web. That was the beginning of nonwovens at 3M, and of our Sasheen-brand decorative ribbon product line, which was subsequently launched in 1948.

Pursuing this technology, other product applications soon followed in the 1950s — products like filament tape and Scotchply-brand reinforced plastics. Then in the late 1950s, a team of scientists came up with the idea of impregnating some nonwoven material with abrasive grain. That was the beginning of 3M's line of Scotchbrite-brand cleaning and finishing materials. This was followed by yet another combination of 3M technologies to enter a new market, 3M Microporebrand surgical tapes, introduced in the early 1960s.

At about the same time, another team of researchers learned how to mold nonwoven fabric. The first application that was tried using this technology was that of making brassiere cups. That idea was ultimately rejected by end-users but paved the way for the application that did catch on, namely, face masks for surgical, industrial, workshop, and cold weather use. Today many thousands of people work more safely because of the variety of masks and respirators produced by 3M's Occupational Health and Safety Products Division.

The list goes on. Working with nonwoven webs got 3M experimenting with fibers. In the early 1970s, a group of process engineers doing fiber extrusion discovered that when large fibers are made out of polyvinyl chloride, the fibers become curly. That was an interesting, but worthless, observation, until, through brainstorming, a group of development engineers and marketing people came up with the idea of bonding them to a backing. That was the launch of the popular Nomad-brand floor mats.

The list of nonwoven products continues to grow and includes such products as Buf-Puf–brand skin cleaning pads, Thinsulate-brand microporous microfiber insulation, which was featured in the 1988 Winter Olympic Games, and a new type of elastic tape.

Commitment to new business development and technology innovation through access to and understanding of customer needs in multiple markets, access to multiple technologies, and the willingness to experiment are the key enabling factors for 3M's success in commercializing new materials.

NOTES

1. Presentation by Joel Barker, Infinity Limited, Inc., at 3M Executive Training Course.
2. Presentation by Ralph Katz, MIT, at 3M Technical Council, September 14, 1987, St. Paul, Minnesota.

IV ENTREPRENEURIAL MANAGEMENT IN TELECOMMUNICATIONS

10 NEW PRODUCT DEVELOPMENT IN TELECOMMUNICATIONS: INNOVATIVE SPIRIT AND STRATEGIC VISION — THE ESSENTIAL INGREDIENTS

Michael L. Bandler

Technology-based industries in California are no strangers to innovation and entrepreneurship; in California we have excelled in industries such as microelectronics, aerospace, biotechnology, electronics manufacturing, diversified manufacturing, agriculture, financial services, and telecommunications.

Innovative spirit and strategic vision are two essential ingredients in the development of technology. A creative spirit — incorporating both risk-seeking and curiosity — is at the heart of a researcher's drive to stretch beyond perceived limits and create new technological solutions. Innovation thrives in a "fail-safe" atmosphere where people explore, take risks, and at times, "fail." Innovation challenges industries to accept failure as part of the path to success.

While innovation is essential to technology development, so too is strategic vision. A vision provides us with a picture of a desirable future, and it challenges technology to take us there. A vision is key for a researcher, as it focuses creative energy, energy that might otherwise have been scattered and thus rendered ineffective. A vision is essential, for in showing us a destination, it often suggests various paths. If we don't know where we're going, how are we going to get there?

Both innovation and strategic vision are interdependent components in technology development at Pacific Bell. With the divestiture of American Telephone and Telegraph (AT&T), the Bell Operating

Companies (BOCs) found themselves in a new competitive environment. Rather than receive both business and technology direction from AT&T, they had to chart their own course. The BOCs had to become keenly aware of their customers' telecommunication wants and needs, as well as of the strengths and weaknesses of their competitors. They had to incorporate this new market awareness into their goals. At Pacific Bell one of our six commitments is, "We are customer-focused," and one of our guiding principles is to "continuously provide superior relative value to our customers, at a reasonable cost." Providing that superior value to our customers is where technology comes into play.

Technology affords the capability to meet customer needs. With divestiture, the BOCs began moving from a position of passive technology transfer — that is, of *receiving technology* — to a proactive technology stance. They began developing the capability to influence and participate in the research and development of technology and communications application.

Today, the BOCs have several options for developing technology, and one important resource is Bellcore. Bellcore was created after divestiture and is to the BOCs what Bell Labs is to AT&T. Bellcore provides support in areas such as planning, marketing, and applied research and is jointly owned by the BOCs. To enhance communication between the BOCs and Bellcore, staff exchanges are common; the staff at Bellcore works at the BOCs, and representatives from the BOCs do research at Bellcore. BOCs influence technology development at Bellcore by directing research based on their specific technology goals.

Another technology resource is internal assessment and R&D departments. At NYNEX there is Science and Technology; at US West there is Information Systems; and at Pacific Bell we have the Technology Department. As BOCs focus on meeting the needs of their region, they differ in the amount of resources allocated to internal R&D and in their R&D goals.

At Pacific Bell, we also encourage the research and development of technology through alliances with universities and with other R&D institutions. At UC Berkeley we are funding circuit and packet data networks, and at Stanford we are funding research in the Communications Satellite Planning Center. At Cal Tech we are funding research in the Integrated Services Digital Network (ISDN) traffic management, local loop digital optimization, and ISDN image compression.

We are also involved in business alliances with companies for projects such as the development of network software.

These alliances serve the purpose of both meeting our customers' telecommunication needs and, equally important, keeping California competitive in terms of the global economy. The following is a summary of the BOCs' various R&D options.

R&D Options for the BOC

Bellcore	A research institution jointly owned by the BOCs
Internal R&D	Internal departments in the individual BOCs
Strategic alliances	Alliances with universities and other R&D institutions.

INNOVATIVE SPIRIT AND PROJECT VICTORIA

In the early days of divestiture, Pacific Bell faced a challenge. Our organization had to quickly develop a new and better way to respond to market needs. With an innovative spirit and newfound excitement, we did just that.

The Challenge

Our Marketing Department came to the Technology Department on several occasions, requesting that we address a variety of customer needs. Customers wanted alarm systems that wouldn't require an extra physical line. They wanted access to the packet network for data, additional voice channels, and services such as home banking and energy management.

The Response

The Technology Department responded with "Project Victoria," and it was a special project for a variety of reasons. Rather than having any one area be fully responsible for Project Victoria, the project team was interdepartmental, consisting of highly skilled people from several departments: Technology, Operations, Legal, and Marketing.

Team members had the flexibility to chart their own course and work without guidelines; they assumed a lot of risk and individual responsibility. The team was resourceful, and rather than attempt to develop a wholly new technology, they extended the capabilities of the existing local loop. Project Victoria transformed the existing local loop into a multiplexed digital transmission pathway. This technology provided customers access to seven simultaneous channels — two voice, one medium-speed data, and four low-speed data — over a single telephone line.

Working within constraints, the project team created new ways to utilize the current state of technology. As a result of their approach, we were able to bring Victoria to a technical trial very quickly; the project start date was March 1984, and the technical trial was made in April 1986.

For Pacific Bell, Project Victoria embodied an innovative spirit. Its interdepartmental nature, emphasis on creativity, flexibility for team members, and resultant responsibility reflected the changing times.

STRATEGIC VISION

Whereas an innovative spirit is essential in creating new technology, there's also a planned component. Innovative and creative technology must take place within the context of a strategic vision; Project Victoria, and projects like it, do not stand alone. They all bring us closer to our vision of the future network.

That vision at Pacific Bell is a fully digital network comprised of entirely optical components capable of effectively transporting and enhancing voice, data, and visual intelligence in an integrated fashion. It will be both integrated and intelligent. Its major characteristics are listed below. Our goal at Pacific Bell is to provide, in a cost-effective manner, the benefits of the Information Age to all Californians.

Major Characteristics of the Future Network

• *Self-healing and instant service.* Customers will receive instant service, and the network can diagnose and correct any of its problems

- *Accessibility is its hallmark.* Customers will have access to the integrated or ISDN network through a single connection, rather than through multiple cables; service providers will also have easy access, making services cost-effective
- *Customer control/flexibility.* Customers can reconfigure the network for more or different services; the network will be flexible, and customers can customize it for their own needs

Moving Toward Our Vision

In order to bring about this vision and achieve the goals of the future network, we need to provide interoffice facilities in a digital manner. Pacific Bell has been deploying digital technology for over twenty years, and currently approximately 85 percent of our interoffice facilities are based on digital technology. In recent years, this deployment has been expanded to include the use of digital technology to provide switching functions (both circuit and packet) and to upgrade the local loop.

Technology and Customer Needs

Technology development raises an important question for the BOCs: Should technological capabilities drive the public network or should satisfying our customers' needs — even if those needs require only the current network capabilities — be the driving force for our technological development?

At Pacific Bell, we look not to leading-edge technology but to the right technology for the market. We want the technology that will be cost-effective and will bring services that customers desire and need, at the appropriate place, price, and time. We view technology not in a vacuum, but in a market context. Technology is the solution, and we see this solution within the context of our customers' needs.

Network Modernization Strategy

We envision our network modernization as an evolutionary process resulting from the continued use of digital technology within existing integrated digital networks. Our strategy consists of three phases:

Transition.   This phase involves the process of preparing the network for a graceful evolution to an ISDN. It consists of the continued deployment of digital technology — extending digital capability to provide both switching and transmission functions — and the introduction of transition services, such as packet-switched data and customer control network management.

Intermediate.   The second phase involves initial offerings of ISDN-based services in selected areas; it envisions the creation of "ISDN islands" and the availability of ISDN-compatible equipment for both customers and network providers.

Mature.   The final phase will see the interconnection of the ISDN islands deployed in the intermediate phase and will result in national and international ISDNs. This phase allows both network providers and service providers to quickly introduce new services. At this phase, customers will realize the benefits of the Information Age. The phases in our network modernization strategy are summarized below.

Phases in Network Modernization Strategy

Transition:
Continued deployment of digital technology
Extended digital capability to provide both switching and transmission function
Transition services such as packet-switched data and customer control network management

Intermediate:
Initial offerings of ISDN-based services in selected areas, or "islands"
Availability of ISDN-compatible equipment for customers and network providers

Mature:
Interconnection of ISDN islands
Benefits of Information Age to all customers

Industry Standards

Industry standards are a key component in our network vision. It is by adhering to standards that public exchange networks make the network both cost-effective and easily accessible to customers and vendors. Pacific Bell is an active member of the Consultive Committee for International Telephone and Telegraph (CCITT) and is involved in designing standards.

Bellcore has an important role in our network strategy. Bellcore is our representative at many of the standards committee meetings, and in addition, our vision of the future marketplace sets a focus for Bellcore's R&D. Through open communication and technology transfer and transformation — that is, taking the research from Bellcore and making it our own — we benefit from Bellcore's applied research.

In developing new technology, innovative spirit and creative spirit are channeled and focused by a strategic vision of the future network, a vision employing the right technology for intelligently planned progress.

11 LINKING TECHNOLOGY AND NEW MARKETS IN TELECOMMUNICATIONS

E. Oran Brigham

There is no single strategy for transferring technology to the marketplace. Indeed, a number of variables must be carefully analyzed and integrated in developing a company's strategy for commercializing each new technology. In addition to the technology itself, such factors as customer demand, consumer habits, competition, product cost, and luck are all factors that determine business strategy. A highly successful business is one in which management's judgment correctly postures the company to take advantage of all these strategic planning factors. In this chapter my objective is to describe strategies that Avantek, a high-technology company, has successfully used for commercializing a sophisticated gallium arsenide material technology.

GALLIUM ARSENIDE

Gallium arsenide is a material that can be used to produce semiconductor transistors. One generally thinks of semiconductor devices as being made from silicon material—personal computers, automobile digital displays, computer systems, digital clocks, video games, and electronic defense systems are all based on silicon semiconductor devices. All of these applications generally operate at speeds less than one million cycles per second (one megahertz) because of limitations of silicon material. However, gallium arsenide material is capable of operating at much higher frequencies.

Semiconductor devices manufactured from gallium arsenide material can be used to transmit radio or electromagnetic signals in the atmosphere at frequencies from one million to over 100 billion cycles per second (100 gigahertz [GHz]). Satellites, radars, communications equipment, television, telephone service, and defense electronics are examples of products in which high-frequency electronics are employed.

Gallium arsenide semiconductor devices are more costly than those made from silicon. Hence, gallium arsenide applications must provide some economic benefit or added value to justify the increased expense. Strategies for commercialization of the technology must take this basic factor into account. As seen from the following cases, each application of this sophisticated technology has its own story and strategy.

HOME SATELLITE TELEVISION

In the late 1970s individuals began purchasing large antenna systems to receive television programs that were being broadcast by satellite. At that time, these systems cost up to $15,000, but they allowed the viewer to receive unedited news reports being transmitted to New York for nightly network news broadcasts, to view movies without paying cable companies, and to view television personalities' "off-air" comments during commercial breaks. (Johnny Carson was frequently mentioned in this context.)

Consumer demand, particularly in rural areas, was strongly a function of price; hence, a classic business study of "elasticity" was the basis for strategy decisions.

To succeed in the marketplace, costs of home systems had to be greatly reduced. One of the keys to reducing system cost was to reduce the size of the antenna. This objective was accomplished by improving and reducing the cost of the high-frequency electronics (4GHz), and improved gallium arsenide technology reduced the size and cost of the antenna. Costs were lowered further as Avantek automated its microwave semiconductor and component manufacturing. Manufacturers of equipment for the satellite terminal reduced their cost as well. Combining all three reductions, costs were reduced by a factor of ten. Home satellite television receiving systems could be bought for $1,000–1,500.

Demand soared, from thousands of systems per year to one million systems per year. Avantek, because of its gallium arsenide technology, was the number-one supplier in the world, with a 60 percent market share.

Our strategy had worked – the consumer could receive over 100 channels of television for less than $1,500. With the large demand, foreign suppliers became more numerous, but our investment in manufacturing automation and gallium arsenide technology provided us with a competitive edge.

But strategies are not forever. In October 1985, the movie networks began scrambling their television signals broadcast by satellites. Consumer television screens became blank on these scrambled channels. Although fewer than 10 percent of the available channels were affected, consumer interest fell sharply, and the market collapsed in a period of less than thirty days. Pricing was not an issue – there simply was no demand. Inventory levels were high, and Avantek eventually wrote off three months of inventory – 120,000 units and plant assets, at a cost of $8 million.

MICROWAVE TRANSMISSION EQUIPMENT

Many long-distance telephone conversations today are carried across the country by means of microwave radios. These radios use traveling wave tubes to generate the microwave signals that transmit telephone conversations from mountaintop to mountaintop. The system works fine if the tubes are replaced every one or two years. But this continual replacement is obviously quite costly.

Enter gallium arsenide technology. Avantek developed a replacement solid-state amplifier, using gallium arsenide devices that last at least ten years before failing. The business strategy thus was to price the solid-state replacement component so that it would be competitive with the cost of ten years' worth of replacement tubes. Because of the difficulties, and accessibility costs, of getting to many mountaintops, long-distance telephone companies will readily upgrade their systems with solid-state amplifiers to reduce maintenance. As a result of this new technology, today Avantek is the leading supplier of gallium arsenide amplifiers to the telecommunications industry.

DEFENSE ELECTRONICS

Military communications, radar, aircraft countermeasure systems, navigation equipment, missiles, and aircraft avionics generally operate at high frequencies. Older systems are based on tube equipment similar to that described in the previous example. The systems were larger, had poor reliability, and were limited in capability. Gallium arsenide was the new technology that promised to upgrade the performance of numerous defense electronics systems. A large number of new products were waiting to be engineered using this new technology.

Avantek began developing microwave components based on gallium arsenide technology for the defense marketplace in the early 1970s. Since that time, the company's strategy has been to supply defense customers with small, lightweight, and reliable products that provide a significant increase in system capabilities. Today almost every defense electronics system that operates at high frequency utilizes products based on Avantek's gallium arsenide technology. This was a major new market that the new technology opened.

MICROWAVE INSTRUMENTATION

The application of gallium arsenide to microwave instrumentation is an example of a strategy based on "anticipation of need." Avantek products operate at billions of cycles per second, and hence, users of those products require test equipment to design and manufacture equipment incorporating these microwave products. Avantek developed gallium arsenide–based products that can be used by companies that manufacture instruments. Today these products are found in leading instrument manufacturers around the world.

MICROWAVE TRANSMISSION EQUIPMENT

A fundamental law of physics is that the higher the frequency, the larger the amount of information that can be transmitted. Based on this premise, Avantek leveraged its gallium arsenide technology into microwave transmission equipment to relay hundreds of telephone conversations simultaneously. Telephone companies were searching for a means to overcome the problem of almost constant interruption of service because of "down" telephone lines. The new technology allowed telephone companies to replace telephone poles and wire lines in rural areas of the United States. The strategy was one of providing superior telephone service at an affordable price, and the new technology made this possible.

CELLULAR TELEPHONES

Some market opportunities for new technology are more a matter of just plain luck than of superior planning or foresight. For example, Avantek did not decide ten years ago that many individuals would have telephones in their cars and that gallium arsenide technology would be an important component to the commercial success of an emerging mobile telephone market. Other companies had the vision and had planned to use local telephone lines to carry telephone conversations received from automobiles. However, the system has grown so rapidly that an immediate need for microwave transmission equipment was created.

Fortunately, Avantek had the appropriate product at the correct time, as a result of the transmission equipment developments discussed in the previous example. Today almost 50 percent of the cities offering cellular telephone service base these services on Avantek's gallium arsenide technology, and this is a rapidly expanding market. Although other companies had well thought out strategies to provide cellular telephone service and Avantek did not, nevertheless Avantek benefited from having advanced microwave transmission technology in place to serve this new market development.

FUTURE APPLICATIONS OF GALLIUM ARSENIDE

In satellite communication systems, cost is determined by the size of the antenna and the electronics. Five years ago, a satellite terminal cost at least $250,000. If frequency is increased, then antenna size can be decreased. Satellite terminals based on gallium arsenide technology can now be manufactured for about $10,000. This cost will drop to $3,000–5,000 in five years. When this event occurs, customers will enter credit card information into a satellite terminal to purchase gasoline at a service station. The satellite will relay the request to a central processing and billing site somewhere in the United States. A credit card check (elimination of bad credit card charges will pay for the system) will be performed, and the gasoline pump will be activated for the customer. When the customer completes the transaction, another satellite terminal will debit, within seconds, the customer's bank balance. Credit card "float" will be another relic of the "good old days."

Future ultrahigh-speed computers will be based on gallium arsenide technology. Major segments of motion pictures will be computer-generated because computer speeds will allow the simulation of natural events so realistic that detection of what is "real" from what is computer-generated will be impossible.

Automobiles and trucks will someday be equipped with navigation and self-positioning equipment. A display will provide direction information to assist the driver in traveling to an input destination. Trucking firms will be able to constantly monitor truck movement throughout the United States, enhancing the overall efficiency of the transportation industry.

Gallium arsenide technology will be a key component of each of these developments. In each case, the factors most important to a successful product must be incorporated into the planning strategy.

SUMMARY

As discussed, strategies for taking technology to the marketplace are based on many factors. Common to all strategies is a focus on the customer and his needs. Avantek is a superior company in taking technology to the marketplace because of a strong customer focus. The twenty-one year compounded growth rate of the company is almost 40 percent annually. This growth has been achieved by a multiplicity of strategies—no two of which are exactly the same. Each of the market segments that Avantek serves has been selected so that the company's microwave technology (primarily based on gallium arsenide) places the company in an innovative and leadership position. Avantek has over 700 products that are used by more than 2,000 customers, ranging from aerospace contractors who need space-qualified gallium arsenide transistors to business firms requiring an installed, ready-to-operate digital microwave telecommunications network. The company is generally recognized as the premier U.S. supplier of microwave products.

Innovation, entrepreneurial management, customer focus, and strong technology—these are the essential elements to continuing business success in taking new technology to the marketplace.

V ENTREPRENEURIAL MANAGEMENT IN INFORMATION SYSTEMS

12 COMMERCIALIZING DEFENSE TECHNOLOGIES

Charles H. Shorter

TRW Inc. is a diversified international company that provides hundreds of products and services with a high technological or engineering content to electronics, defense, space, information systems, automotive, and energy markets. It employs more than 75,000 people, many with sophisticated technical expertise, at about 300 locations in twenty-five countries.

Throughout its eighty-five-year history, TRW has demonstrated a pronounced flexibility and willingness to change — to reshape itself to pursue the most promising opportunities in growth markets. In its key businesses, TRW is either the leader or near-leader, and the company is embarking on programs to strengthen those positions even further.

In pursuit of those objectives, TRW will continue to draw on a considerable technological reservoir — technologies such as microelectronics, advanced manufacturing processes, electronic and mechanical controls, advanced materials, lasers, avionics, signal and image processing, information processing, and software development. To keep in the forefront of these prime technologies, the company has performed about $7.3 billion of research and development — about 83 percent of it customer-funded — and has invested about $1.8 billion in facilities and equipment during the past five years.

As part of this process of change, TRW is constantly exploring ways to commercialize its defense expertise. Many corporations that have attempted the crossover, including TRW, have failed because the two

115

sectors have different needs and cultures. Ruben Mettler, TRW chairman and CEO, recently stated:

> We've been struggling and sweating and wrestling for years to use our defense and space technology in commercial markets. That's a tough proposition when it comes to hardware. Our best success in making that transfer has been in computer-based information systems.[1]

Commercial information systems and services has recently become the most profitable and fastest growing part of the company. Technology transfer has been an element of this success, and TRW is continuing to give special emphasis to the transfer of advanced information technology from defense and space programs.

This chapter describes TRW's motivation for technology transfer as well as the process, results, and lessons learned from four examples. In two examples, we have a clear business need, or pull, for technology. The other examples involve the process of converting technology push into market pull.

MOTIVATION FOR TRANSFER

New technology, creatively applied to a business problem or a market need, can lead to significant competitive advantage, both for the end-user of that technology and for the purveyor of it. The key to success is filling a need in the marketplace. A commercial customer buys benefits, not technology. They want solutions to business problems, not innovation for the sake of innovation. The focus of TRW's technology transfer activity is applying the appropriate technologies to create competitive advantage for both TRW and its customers in the commercial marketplace. Our intent is to transfer technology to our commercial businesses from our defense and space businesses.

THE COMMERCIAL BUSINESSES

The TRW Information System Group (ISG), established in mid-1984 by combining internal units that serve commercial markets, has about doubled in size since then and entered 1987 with an annual sales rate approaching $500 million. The business is expected to continue growing at rates of about 20 percent annually over the next several years, as part of an industry that should enjoy a growth rate possibly twice that of the overall economy.

The growth of the information systems and services business reflects a fundamental change in the way people increasingly obtain the facts they need and want. This information now comes primarily from electronic data bases. Indeed, widespread use of small computers and other electronic systems has increased significantly the access to electronically generated information. The resulting ISG businesses serve both consumers and financial institutions.

In the ISG businesses — in credit, marketing, and real estate information services; in equipment servicing and training; and in systems development and integration — success hinges on TRW's expertise in system analysis, software development, on-line data services, electronics, and project management.

To continue to succeed in such a high-growth industry, TRW faces a three-pronged challenge: (1) to keep its costs down and provide additional benefits in its existing businesses; (2) to rapidly expand its existing information systems and services businesses; and (3) to use its data bases and technologies to develop new information products and services tailored to the most important needs of customers.

TRW's response to these challenges is to identify a need, or a market pull, for advanced information technologies. An environment and attitude of "market-pull versus technology-push" is a significant factor in successful technology transfer.

Generally speaking, there are two types of information technologies. *Product technology* is the know-how for designing a particular product, such as a data-base management system; a queuing algorithm at the heart of communication switching software; an artificial intelligence algorithm applied to protecting proprietary data bases, or special digital processors for text scanning or network control. *Process technology* is the technology, such as software engineering, productivity tools, or life cycle and project management, that is used in the production and integration of software modules into a software system or total system.

THE DEFENSE AND SPACE BUSINESS

In TRW's defense and space efforts, the information systems content of programs employing advanced technologies has grown rapidly in recent years to well over $1 billion per year. TRW has exceptional technological and project management capabilities, which are well suited to complex information system problems, and has long been acknowledged as a leader in defense information systems. TRW's expertise includes creating systems for signal processing, text scanning, secure communications, local area networks, and a wide variety of sophisticated software. The staff of over 10,000 engineering professionals is one of the largest pools of technical talent in the world. *Datamation* has identified TRW as the second largest (behind IBM) software producer in the world.[2] TRW is the only company in the software top ten that is independent of a particular brand of computer hardware. The majority of the software produced is for very demanding, real-time applications. Through the TRW software productivity program, the company's programmers have doubled their individual output since 1980 and expect to double it again by 1990.

In summary, TRW has a large and in-depth base of applicable defense information technologies to draw upon for commercial applications.[3]

THE TECHNOLOGY BRIDGE

To help stimulate more rapid new product development for our commercial customers, we have established an organization within ISG to give special emphasis to the transfer of advanced information systems technology from defense and space programs to commercial applications. To be successful, we had to bridge the gap between the needs and cultures of the two organizations. A key part of this is organizational commitments to achieve or facilitate business benefits for both sides from technology transfer.[4]

First, we knew that technology alone does not sell in the commercial market. A commercial customer wants the solutions and benefits that technology can provide for a competitive advantage, but it must be packaged appropriately, based on market research, pilot or prototype

evaluations, manufacturing, sales, distribution, training, and maintenance. Technology is typically a small part of the total cost and schedule in getting a product to market. In other words, technology alone
will not ensure the successful development of a product. This is often
overlooked in the movement of technology to the marketplace and is
described later in more detail in our example of the local area network
business.

This understanding led to the new organization, the Technology
Systems Organization (TSO), which has been staffed with both technologists and businessmen. We preferred "Renaissance men" who
were skilled and experienced in both disciplines. To attract this type of
individual, the organization was structured so as to maintain a focus on
creating new commercial system development and integration businesses, during which process technologies would be transferred to the
other ISG commercial businesses, for example, the credit and real
estate information services. In other words, it was not strictly a staff
organization to facilitate technology transfer.

The commercial system integration market is a large and growing
market. The transferable technologies and processes are, to a large
degree, common to designing, developing, and integrating both defense and commercial information systems. Technologies for the data-
base services businesses are typically a subset of those required for full
systems development and integration. TSO uses the technology for
commercial systems efforts and serves as the "bridge" organization to
the remainder of ISG.

Common technology needs across the entire organization were necessary but not sufficient for successful transfers. Other significant
factors were a corporate commitment to the transfer process, vision-
ary leadership to see that it was accomplished, and a market-driven
attitude on all sides. The organization responsible for the transfer was
staffed with executives qualified to understand the businesses and
technologies and with senior personnel possessing strong commercial
experience and appropriate technical backgrounds. It was important
to establish good working relationships between the organizations
where the technology originated and the organizations it was being
transferred to. This took time, understanding of each other's business,
trust, and a demonstration of support. This was facilitated by the
full-time transfer of skilled personnel between organizations. Approximately half of the TSO staff, including myself, were originally from

the defense business. The remainder were from other parts of TRW and from external commercial businesses. Finally, achieving business benefits and then recognizing and rewarding performance fueled the transfer process.

CASE STUDIES OF SUCCESSFUL COMMERCIALIZATION

In the discussion that follows, you will see examples of upgraded or modified technology flowing back to the original organization.

1. Commercial Credit

In consumer credit information, TRW continues to hold a leading market share. Credit reports are supplied to financial organizations such as banks, mortgage companies, retailers, and credit card companies. TRW's data network, one of the world's largest, processes more than 75 million consumer credit reports a year. Recently enlarged, the network now covers consumers in all fifty states. The on-line data base has credit information on more than 130 million individuals. Transactions occur at rates of 45,000 per hour. Customer access is provided in seconds. The update process involves adding an additional 1.2 billion characters of information a month. Also, TRW supplies business credit information about business entities and markets portions of its credit data base to firms that wish to target particular groups of prospective customers.

An example of transferring both product and process technology is the use of an expert system for data security in our consumer credit data base. We call the project DISCOVERY.[5] There was a clear business need in our large credit data-base business. Hackers, private investigators, and criminals have found several effective methods of acquiring passwords and instructions to access computer systems. These individuals don't have to be in collusion with the person who is the legitimate user of the password. The hacker will "dumpster dive" to derive access instructions from a legitimate subscriber's trash. The private investigator will phone the custodian of the password and gain this data through subterfuge, pretending to be someone who should already have this knowledge. The criminal will use either of these means to gain access instructions and passwords to your system.

Our system, like most automated systems, has the capability to lock out a hacker or unauthorized individual attempting to log on with an invalid password. The challenge was to identify the impostor who has access to log-on identifiers and inquiry formats. Most illegal use of valid access codes for a system go undetected unless the condition is brought to the attention of the system manager by the legitimate system user. An ability to detect unauthorized use of legitimate access parameters was required.

TRW's goal was to review all daily inquiry activity and detect those inquiries made by an unauthorized individual. The system called DIS-COVERY must process more than 400,000 inquiries per day, from a potential base of 120,000 customer access codes. At many of these locations, several persons are authorized to access the system.

The facilitating organization, TSO, was involved from the original problem definition. It was clear that expert systems were a potential solution. TSO was aware of expert systems research on similar "pattern matching" algorithms being conducted in the defense organization. TSO arranged for the assignment of a principal investigator from the defense organization to prove or disprove the technology application. After a prototype solution was completed, it was evaluated by a team led by the commercial credit organization. The prototype was a success, and the production system is currently being developed. Individuals from TSO also performed a project review role.

We have also achieved an additional unexpected benefit. The customer usage patterns that have been developed as a result of DIS-COVERY are the most detailed, up-to-the-minute marketing data we have available on our customers. These patterns provide a current and complete picture of our customers' credit report purchasing characteristics. We have developed a pattern of what services they're buying, when they're buying these services, and the transaction configuration.

An outgrowth of this purchasing pattern is the data it provides to our risk analysis efforts. Through further analysis, we can see the direction in which service and access characteristics are evolving. As our service lines and access methods evolve, we will have access methodologies in place to provide an even more secure environment.

The net result for technology transfer was that expert system algorithms, software engineering, and architecture skills were successfully transferred to produce DISCOVERY.

2. Commercial Real Estate Information Services

In real estate information, TRW is one of the largest suppliers of data to the home equity lending market. The business supplies title, tax, and transaction history, as well as appraisal information services and automated systems to more than 2,000 customers in the mortgage, finance, and real estate industries. Its computerized reports on properties can be furnished anywhere in the nation. Presently over 12,000 real estate appraisals per month are provided to our customers.

The second example involves the TRW Appraisal Services (TAS). The real estate appraisal process can be considered an "art," practiced by a select few "experts." That is not to say that there aren't guidelines mandated by the marketplace and the government. However, given the identical property, in the identical neighborhood, five appraisers could come up with different appraised values for that property and would take several weeks to do it. The challenge was to apply technology to this process to produce a consistent, quality appraisal in a timely and cost-effective manner. The nature of the problem itself is an ideal candidate for technology transfer. It is a labor-intensive and subjective process, performed with limited resources. Successful automation of this process could "revolutionize" the industry and place TRW in a position of significant competitive advantage.

The methodology followed and the technology employed on this project are not themselves revolutionary or leading-edge. The approach taken was similar to that used on many high-priority and complex defense projects. A combined TSO and TAS team was formed, representing both the developers and the users. After analysis of the problem, the anticipated benefits were estimated to be significant enough to warrant a pilot project. It is important to note that it was viewed as a pilot. The risk was understood and accepted. It also held implications for the design and development process. Rapid development of a working prototype was paramount. Proof-of-concept as quickly as possible was a critical prerequisite to the real estate business organization. Bells and whistles could be added to the system later.

The traditional top-down structural methodological approach was not appropriate; instead, an iterative approach was employed. Iterative design shortens the development process by using the system itself as the primary communication tool between developer and user. The user reviews a working model of the system rather than design documentation, and modifications are implemented in the subsequent iterations of the system. Iterative design is not applicable to all development projects, nor to all organizations, but it does embody the innovative attitude of the technology transfer culture.

From the outset, rapid development and productivity were key criteria in the technology selection process. In addition, flexibility and portability were also viewed as critical, since the prototype evolves as the processing requirements—and eventual production environment—are better understood. Special resources from the defense organization were used for the hardware/software selection process. As difficulties arose in the automation of specific pieces of the appraisal process, the innovative nature of TRW again came to light. Rather than choosing not to automate that piece of the process, or choosing to automate with traditional technologies that would have provided less than an optimal solution, TRW chose to apply expert system technology to the problem. The new automated appraisal product is currently being introduced to the marketplace. It was the combination of an innovative attitude and the technology resources of both the defense and commercial sides of TRW that provided a technology transfer solution to this business problem.

New Commercial Systems and Product Development

In the commercial systems integration arena, TRW provides capabilities that involve managing automated information projects from start to finish. That means designing systems, installing hardware and software, running data bases, and providing networks, training, maintenance, and service. A major TRW business unit in this area provides information processing systems and consulting services, records management systems, and systems for handling checks, credit card drafts and payments, and automated bank teller transactions. Those systems, based on a patented digital image process, speed the transmittal of financial data, without the burden of paper documentation.

During the past year, the defense and space organization introduced an information processing system with strong defense potential called the TRW Fast Data Finder™ (FDF) system.[6] It will enable users to scan raw data simultaneously for nearly 500 different kinds of complex search requests, at a rate of more than 7 million characters a second—the equivalent of six 500-page novels. The government plans to use FDF for statistical, trend, and intelligence analysis, battlefield management, and message routing.

Concurrently with the FDF technology development in the defense and space organization, the commercial organization did initial market research to determine the commercial market and customer need for a rapid text search system. It was an exciting technology, and possible commercial customers included banks, securities brokers, and others involved in data-intensive, analytical activities in which speed is important. A small team of individuals from the defense area transferred to the commercial organization. The objective of this phase was to support further market research and to construct a prototype for exploring commercial applications.

This phase has now been completed. A prototype of a small workstation-based FDF for the commercial market was developed. Liaison between the two organizations resulted in additional workstation prototypes being developed by the commercial group for use by the defense organization in defense applications ("backward technology transfer"). Several exciting commercial applications were further defined, some in new marketplaces. The most promising are progressing at different speeds into the next phase—prototype evaluation in a customer's environment. The following phase, development and production, will be started in the near future, after market and financial evaluations are completed.

The incremental approach was taken, based upon previous TRW experiences. Taking new technology products to new marketplaces is very high-risk and achieving a high enough return to compensate for this risk requires unusual clarity and perception of market timing, demand, and cost to commercialize. Additionally, we have learned that a product development of this type should be of strategic importance to the company and, once started, should be rapidly executed and strongly financed. Available market position should be quickly developed before established competitors can respond.

4. Commercial Information Networks

The Information Networks Division (IND) of TRW designs, manufactures, and markets high-performance local area network (LAN) systems.[7] LANs connect data processing equipment, such as computers, printers, terminals, and PCs, from different manufacturers. IND is focused on the general-purpose office LAN segment for both federal government (DOD) and large commercial systems customers. Many large systems have been successfully completed. The product line is now one of the most complete in the industry, with a combination of TRW products licensed from a number of other companies in complementary segments of the LAN industry.

TRW developed the LAN technology as a result of a number of government programs and extensive in-house research and development. Based upon a study of the technology and potential market, IND was started in January 1985 as an operation unit of the company. The technology was transferred by approximately thirty individuals who moved to the new organization. The plan was to build a product line with development, manufacturing, sales, and support around the technology.

Initial product design problems caused difficulties in completing installations for our large customers. Satisfactory completion of some major systems was particularly difficult because early estimates of the effort to transform the LAN from defense technology into a marketable product were optimistic and were added to the normal growing pains of a new organization. Start-up problems in the first year were overcome as the organization grew from thirty to ninety people, product designs were stabilized, quantity shipments were made, and all major installations were successfully completed. Despite these initial problems, revenues have grown at the rate of approximately 40 percent per year and are expected to continue at this rate for the next few years.

STRATEGIES FOR SUCCESS

Along the way, a number of valuable lessons were learned regarding technology transfer.

First, products and technology are clearly not synonymous. Products satisfy a buyer need and must be capable of being developed, manufactured, and distributed to buyers, as well as supported after the sale. We found that sales could be made based on description of technology, but customers would remain dissatisfied until working solutions to their problems could be delivered and maintained. Devices that did what their designers expected were complex enough that few people could figure out how to use them without extensive help, and customers were not provided adequate diagnostics when failures did occur. These problems were solved by extensive documentation, by customer support made available through a toll-free call to a "trouble desk" manned by friendly, responsive, and knowledgeable people, and by capable instructors in user training. All of these product distribution and support functions are absolutely critical to the success of product business and do not come from "technology transfer."

Second, mass-produced products such as LANs must be reproducible at competitive prices. In the highly competitive LAN market, this requires sound designs capable of being mass-produced using off-the-shelf parts with a minimum of adjustments. This became obvious when we found it required advanced-degree electrical engineers and technicians to build, tune, and maintain our units and related equipment. We found that technical people who were accustomed to research and development had little appreciation for the design discipline required in using industry-standard, off-the-shelf components, or for manufacturing simplicity. "Why keep it simple when elegance is so much more challenging," is an appropriate description of this attitude.

On the other hand, we would never have had a product without pioneering efforts of the technologists. It took a different discipline to turn the "technology" into a shippable product with satisfactory gross margin (necessary for a profitable business). Prototypes and proofs-of-concept are only the first steps in the total product development process. This is necessary, but by no means sufficient, for success.

The last but perhaps most significant lesson regards people, their experience, and their motivation. Transfer of people with experience and training in a technology development environment to a product business presents challenges as extensive as those associated with transfer of the technology itself. "Technologists" often fail to find the follow-through necessary to complete products that meet customer needs to be either worthwhile or satisfying. One example is second-sourcing parts (to ensure that plenty are available when production starts and to reduce production costs when suppliers compete for business). Another example is providing both engineering and user documentation. A typical response was, "But that's a manufacturing problem," or, "That's a routine design — get the draftsman to do it."

In summary, technology is very important. However, it must be combined with sound business planning and qualified, experienced product development and marketing personnel to succeed in the business. A commercial customer buys benefits, not technology.

SUMMARY OF TRW'S TECHNOLOGY COMMERCIALIZATION EXPERIENCES

Our recent success in technology transfer is largely due to experience gained in past projects involving technology transfer. Highlights of this experience are:

- An understanding that a customer buys benefits, not technology.
- A market pull is best created by competitive commercial business situations. This market pull in the receiving organization not only contributes to the commitment, but it gives an immediate focus to the use of the technology.
- Transfer is more likely when a large and in-depth base of defense technologies and technologists are available to meet both the commercial and defense market needs.
- Technology transfer must have the full commitment of everybody involved — not just top management, but the worker levels and everybody in between, in both the sending and receiving organizations.
- You have to transfer not only the technology but some of the people responsible for technology. This not only moves the knowledge, it ensures that the receiving organization gets a fair measure of automatic commitment.
- Technology can provide a competitive advantage, but technology alone will not ensure the successful development of a product. It must be packaged with market research, pilot or prototype evaluations, manufacturing, sales, distribution, training, and maintenance. Technology is typically a small part of the total cost and schedule in getting a product to market.

NOTES

1. Ruben Mettler, "Can They Keep It Up?" *Forbes*, 9 February 1987, p. 46.
2. "Top 100," *Datamation* (June 1986).
3. "For TRW, Diversity Breeds Success," *Computer Decisions* (August 1986): 34.
4. TRW, 1986 Annual Report (March).
5. "Discovery: An Expert System in the Commercial Data Security Environment," Federation of Information Processors, Technical Committee No. 2 on Computer Security, Monte Carlo: December 1986.
6. "Pipelined for Speed: The Fast Data Finder System,™" *TRW Quest* (Winter 1986–1987).
7. "The Local Network Solution," *TRW Quest* (Winter 1985–1986).

13 TECHNOLOGY COMMERCIALIZATION AT SRI INTERNATIONAL

Richard A. Marciano

SRI is an independent, nonprofit research, development, and consulting organization. We solve problems for business and government worldwide. Most often we create solutions through the development and application of technology.

SRI is sometimes described as a for-hire "skunk works." This is to say that we often carry a project from research through preparation of an operating prototype. This mode of operation is perhaps best illustrated by our relationship a few years ago to the Savin Corporation. We played a key role in developing the Savin-700 series plain-paper copier, which made Savin an important factor in the business copier field at that time. We worked on all aspects of the product line—electronic, mechanical, and chemical. The relationship lasted for ten years; we were, in effect, Savin's R&D lab.

Most companies find it difficult to move a technology product efficiently from research to prototype. It's not at all unusual for turf fights to occur as a product is handed from Research to Design Engineering, to Product Engineering, and then to Production. SRI's structure is different. We form a project team comprising all of the skills and technical disciplines needed to carry a project to completion and the authority to do so.

I personally like the "skunk works" label; however, it diverts from the fact that some 18 percent of our revenues come from basic research.

Another 60 percent of our revenues comes from our work in applied research, including the "skunk workery."

The remainder of our revenues come from our worldwide business consulting activities. SRI deals in all aspects of business consulting. Many have noted the difficulty of finding corporations and individuals within corporations who are receptive to innovations. I turn to our Business Consulting Group. Typically, they have the knowledge and contacts and can point me to receptive companies and the right people in the companies. That sort of assistance is very important because new technology is not sold to directors of research, or to corporate patent counsels, or to others who may appear to have nominal responsibility for acquiring outside technology. Instead, technologies are sold to line executives who hold product-line responsibility.

I also use SRI's business group to do market studies. These are often key in planning our technology marketing strategy.

Earlier, I said SRI is nonprofit. I don't want you to get the wrong idea — we do have to make a profit. We have to have funds to invest in people, program development, facilities, and laboratory equipment. SRI is largely a laboratory-based organization. We can't raise capital by selling stock, so we have to maintain earnings. The good news is that we don't have to worry about quarter-to-quarter earnings reports, or about being acquired. We can take a longer view when it seems advisable. To illustrate, SRI has been a leader in artificial intelligence for over twenty-five years, during which time the field has experienced many ups, and as many downs. Artificial intelligence is very popular now, but as far as I know, no profit-making company was able to hang in that long. We did. Today we have one of the four best artificial intelligence research centers in the world.

SRI TECHNOLOGY COMMERCIALIZATION IN 1979

Let's take a look at the SRI technology commercialization program. In 1979, as shown in Figure 13–1, SRI's technology commercialization program consisted entirely of licensing arrangements. Licensing opportunities, however, were not as available as they are today. The NIH ("not-invented-here") attitude was dominant in industry during that era, and SRI's strategy was to use proprietary technologies as a means for obtaining research and development contracts. We simply did not focus much attention on pursuing royalty income or equity arrangements.

At the time, SRI was also strongly opposed to being identified with any product offered for sale commercially by its research clients or licensees. While we believed in our research and technology, the concern was that such identification might be viewed as a product endorsement by SRI.

In retrospect, the concern was unnecessary. One of SRI's primary roles is to transfer technology into public use, and in a free society, "productization" is the most effective way of accomplishing that goal. The practice of hiding SRI's commercial technology developments was also counterproductive. One consequence is that SRI's product contributions are not as well known as they deserve to be.

To illustrate: the "mouse," the pointing device used with many computers, was invented by Doug Englebart at SRI. The mouse is SRI proprietary technology. Every mouse manufacturer pays royalties to SRI. First licensed in 1967, its purpose was to provide inexpensive and ready access to computers at a time when computation cycles, memory, and input/output channels were much more expensive than today. The mouse hit its stride after Steve Jobs, the cofounder of Apple

Figure 13–1.   SRI International, 1979.

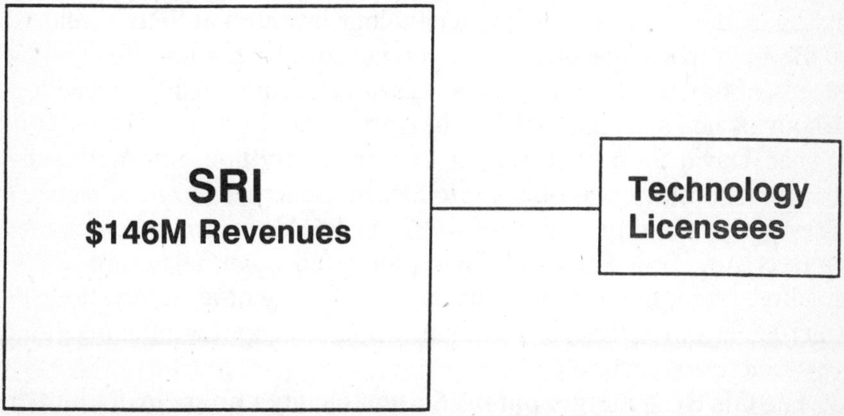

Computer, saw one in use during a visit to the Xerox Palo Alto Research Center. Steve quickly saw the possibilities. He first adopted the mouse for use with the Apple LISA personal computer, and then with the Macintosh. Subsequently, full-page Macintosh ads, placing great emphasis on the mouse, appeared in the *Wall Street Journal* and other publications.

Let's turn to another illustration. Retinal eye surgery performed with a laser photocoagulator is performed to stop retinal bleeding, which often occurs among diabetics, or to reattach a detached retina. Many of the laser photocoagulators used are built by Coherent Radiation Corporation. SRI licensed the basic technology to Coherent in 1974; we believe it has generated well over $100 million in revenues for that company.

SRI TECHNOLOGY COMMERCIALIZATION TODAY

In 1979 we had not ventured into the realms of start-up companies, limited partnerships (R&D and other), strategic alliances, other people's money, batteries of attorneys, and all of the other paraphernalia that plays a role in bringing new products, based upon proprietary technology, to the marketplace.

SRI today is far different than in 1979. The change is summarized in Figure 13–2. As you can see, SRI's activities have been augmented in a major way by those of the David Sarnoff Research Center. In addition, the figure shows SRI's links to several other organizations. Each is engaged in commercializing technology invented at SRI.

Before turning to existing commercialization activities, I'll say a few words about the David Sarnoff Research Center, which became a wholly owned subsidiary of SRI in April of 1987.

The David Sarnoff Research Center, a very fine, internationally known laboratory, was donated to SRI by General Electric Company. Previously, it had been part of RCA. As RCA's central research laboratory, the David Sarnoff Labs pioneered color television, high-fidelity stereo, liquid crystal displays, and many other innovations in microelectronics, lasers, communications, computer memory, and manufacturing technologies.

The GE/RCA merger put the Sarnoff facility's future in doubt. GE has its own corporate research and development center. It didn't

Figure 13–2. SRI International, 1987.

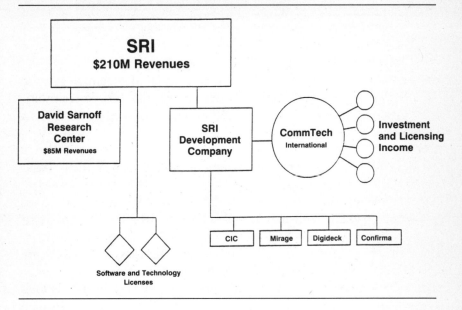

appear feasible to operate two central and geographically separate research facilities.

GE didn't make money by donating the David Sarnoff Research Center to SRI. The donation was made because GE wanted to preserve one of the world's finest research laboratories. SRI was the logical recipient because of its 401(c)(3) nonprofit status, and because its reputation and capabilities are complementary with those of the Sarnoff Center. Undoubtedly, the David Sarnoff Research Center will be another source of entrepreneurial technology commercialization activity by SRI.

PRESENT COMMERCIALIZATION ARRANGEMENTS

SRI uses a variety of arrangements to develop and commercialize its technologies. Product development and commercialization activities are conducted by SRI and a number of other organizations represented above in Figure 13–2. The organizations presently engaged in these activities include:

1. SRI Development Company, a subsidiary of SRI;
2. CommTech International, an independent organization founded to develop and commercialize SRI technologies, having a contract with SRI to do so;
3. four start-up companies: CIC, Mirage, Digideck, and Confirma, each developing products based on particular SRI technology; and,
4. SRI itself, which directly licenses software and some technologies that, for one reason or another, fall outside of CommTech's purview.

I'll describe each of these arrangements and some of the related technologies and products:

SRI Development Company, or DEVCO, as it is sometimes called, is a wholly owned profit-making subsidiary of SRI. DEVCO has two principal functions. It is SRI's link to CommTech International (CI), through which are passed all SRI technologies assigned to CI for commercialization. Also, through its board of directors and management, DEVCO has overview responsibility for SRI relationships with CI and the start-up companies.

CI is a unique entity. It is an investor-funded limited partnership formed in 1982 to develop and commercialize SRI technologies. CI operates under a contract with SRI and DEVCO that gives CI a first right of refusal to substantially all SRI technologies assigned for commercialization. DEVCO owns a one-third limited partnership interest in CI. However, neither DEVCO nor SRI has any CI management role or responsibility. CI is wholly independent of SRI and DEVCO and is operated under the management of its general partner, CommTech International Management Corporation (CIMC). The principals of CIMC founded CI and established CI's relationship with SRI and DEVCO.

It is reasonable to ask why SRI entered into a relationship with CI. Why wasn't it decided instead to manage all commercialization activities internally?

The relationship with CI was desirable for several reasons. Most often, because SRI tends to leading-edge technology, many SRI inventions that appear to offer the greatest commercial promise are at an early stage of development. At this stage, the risk capital needed to develop the product and to bring it to market is typically not available from traditional venture capital sources.

CI faced this dilemma squarely. It offered SRI an approach that provides funding to carry technology development to an advanced state before the technology is licensed or placed in a start-up company. Thus far, CI has raised about $36 million in risk capital from individual and institutional investors. A substantial portion of these funds has been used to support development of promising SRI technologies. You might ask, as others have, why didn't SRI undertake to raise funds itself? The answer is that, as a nonprofit institution, we didn't feel terribly comfortable about raising capital from investors. I personally believe that this feeling may abate gradually as we gain greater experience.

Equally important in the decision to link with CI was SRI's desire for an independent third party to review and choose among the SRI technologies available for commercialization. The decision to proceed with commercialization is not usually an easy one. We believed that an outside body would help maintain a rigorous decision process. This was thought to be particularly important inasmuch as SRI inventors, as will be described later, share in benefits resulting from commercialization.

Some of the technologies that are being commercialized by CI are:

- A recombinant-DNA synthesized growth factor that stimulates wound and burn healing in humans
- An automatic blood pressure measurement and analysis system for ambulatory use by active subjects
- Various compounds of pharmaceutical promise, including anti-tumor and anti-hypertension agents and an oral contraceptive
- A high-performance polymer family of materials, which can be manufactured as fibers or films, characterized by exceptional mechanical properties
- A lightweight flat panel display—for use initially in demanding avionics and computer applications—which is driven by a low-power, "cold" silicon cathode source
- A family of highly sensitive chemical ion and vapor sensors that are microfabricated from silicon

THE START-UP COMPANIES

Let's turn now to the start-up companies. There are four of these: CIC (Communications Intelligence Corporation), Mirage Systems, Digideck, and Confirma Technologies. SRI holds an equity interest in each of these companies, obtained in return for technology and patent rights.

The technology provided by SRI served as a starting point for considerable further development work. In each case, the difficult task of converting the initial technology into useful products was accomplished by the start-up company.

CIC's product is a system that permits a user to communicate with a computer by entering hand-printed text, graphic data, and computer commands with the movement of a pen. The system, called HAND-WRITER, was developed initially for Japanese language computer data entry. Written Japanese consists of several sets of ideographic symbols and over 3,000 characters. A key component of the HAND-WRITER is its extensive ideograph recognition dictionary. The technology appears adaptable to other ideographic languages, such as Chinese or Korean.

The HANDWRITER was originally targeted for sale principally in Japan. The market there has not developed as rapidly as we would like and may reflect resistance to non-Japanese technology in this area of application. CIC has since entered into an agreement that may help to drive the market. The agreement grants nonexclusive manufacturing rights in Japan and sales rights worldwide to Seiko Instruments and Electronics Ltd.

Meanwhile, CIC has directed greater attention to the domestic U.S. market. The HANDWRITER has been adapted to ease the user interface with certain popular PC application programs, including word processing, spread sheet, data base, and graphic applications. For example, by using a specialized template, a user can access the Lotus 1–2–3 spread sheet program through the HANDWRITER.

Mirage Systems produces electronic systems for use in military applications. Its technology and products are highly specialized and complex.

Digideck, which was founded by a predecessor company of CI, is at an earlier stage than the other two companies previously described. The company has digital audio data compression technology, which can be applied to reduce communication costs while maintaining audio high fidelity. In microchip form, the technology may be used in satellite distribution systems, cable television systems, telephone, and other systems that carry digital audio signals.

Confirma Technologies, the last of the start-up companies, is commercializing a personal identification signature technology that originated at SRI. The technology verifies that a signature is authentic through individualistic physical parameters. The process captures the three-dimensional motion and pressures exerted when one signs one's name. It then compares the results with previously recorded data to verify the signer's identification. The motion and pressure parameters are captured either by a pressure-sensitive platen or by a wired and instrumented pen. Use of the pen provides a permanent hard copy signature, which is often necessary for record or legal reasons.

Interestingly, the patents on which Confirma's personal identification technology is based are the same patents that underly the CIC data entry technology. The two companies hold separate licenses for different applications of the same patents.

While the signs are more hopeful than before, the market for personal identification products has yet to unfold. I think that it will, and that ultimately some form of personal signature identification will be used at the point of sale in conjunction with credit and debit cards. In the interim, Confirma is attempting to establish its products in such uses as vault access, check cashing, and other applications in which there is an economic advantage to be gained by reducing the time entailed in the transaction.

SRI's shareholdings in these start-up companies ranges from roughly 14 percent to approximately 46 percent. We are passive shareholders and, except for one temporary assignment, have no management role or responsibility. We very much prefer to be passive and arm's-length. As a matter of SRI policy, we don't want to run commercial companies.

SOFTWARE LICENSING

While SRI is not a producer of commercial software, we often do develop software needed both to support research programs in computer science and artificial intelligence and to provide special capabilities useful in obtaining research contracts. The software that we produce for these purposes is often at an advanced state of development, unlike other technologies available for commercialization. Generally, the software is at the state of the art and is not available from commercial vendors.

Typically, the SRI software has had the benefit of extensive use from very demanding users — our own computer scientists and artificial intelligence researchers. Frequently, we are asked to make such software available to other organizations, and we often do so under license. Many refer to this mode of technology commercialization as the "Hewlett-Packard model" — that is, professionals developing tools needed to accomplish their own work, and finding that they have developed tools of value to other professionals.

Some of the software packages* licensed by SRI are:

1. MultiNet Plus™: A set of networking tools that provides TCP/IP and other protocols, and an electronic mail system and server
2. Gister™: An expert system shell based on evidential reasoning technology
3. Peri™: An expert system shell based on procedural reasoning
4. Grasper II™: An interactive system for constructing and using graphs as a "friendly" and efficient user interface with Gister, Peri, and many other software packages
5. TEAM™: A natural language management system for accessing data bases
6. ImagCalc™: A set of tools for processing and manipulating images interactively
7. SuperSketch™: A three-dimensional solid modeling and graphics manipulation system for use interactively

I tend to devote attention to licensing software because it offers immediate financial results. Current results are important in sustaining interest in the overall longer term commercialization program. While other technologies, if successful, offer promise of greater financial returns than software, such returns are far in the future, given the time typically required to develop and move technology to market.

*MultiNet Plus, Gister, Peri, Grasper II, Team, ImagCalc, and SuperSketch are trademarks of SRI International.

UNDERLYING FACTORS

As you have seen, SRI has adopted a variety of entrepreneurial approaches in order to better move its proprietary technologies to the marketplace. The change to greater entrepreneurship was triggered, and continues to be fostered, by several factors.

First, William F. Miller became president and CEO of SRI in 1979. In addition to a distinguished career as provost, vice president of research, and faculty member at Stanford University, Dr. Miller also brought a venture capital background to SRI. In 1969 he was one of the founders of the Mayfield Fund, one of the earliest of the successful venture funds. While he resigned his partner's role in 1971 to avoid any possibility of conflict with his Stanford responsibilities, Dr. Miller continued his contacts and interest in the venture field.

A second factor was enactment in 1980 of the Bayh-Dole Act (P.L. 96–517), possibly one of the most enlightened of legislative acts. The legislation assigns patent rights to technologies developed under U.S. government grants and contracts to universities and nonprofits. Why? Legislators and government policymakers have learned that, unless patent rights are assigned, there is little chance that such inventions will ever be marketed, and potential economic benefit to the nation is likely to be lost.

Note that the government does retain royalty-free access to the invention for government use. Also note that recipients of patent rights are required to take responsibility for commercializing the technology.

A third factor has been the greater availability of risk capital. This phenomenon has received considerable publicity and attention.

Finally, staff considerations played an important part in SRI's increased emphasis on technology commercialization. Creative engineers and scientists are strongly motivated by a need to see their inventions put into practical use. A related consideration is what I call the "Silicon Valley Syndrome." In the high-tech corridors of the United States, it's almost expected that engineers and scientists will get involved with high-risk ventures. And not all are suited to doing so. For every successful entrepreneurial technologist, there are many more who invest five years or so of their lives in start-up ventures without achieving their dreams. Many people try it, but very few pull it off.

SRI wanted to provide its staff with a way to participate in the entrepreneurial experience and to share in the rewards without having to leave SRI if they didn't care to. Thus, we have a royalty-sharing policy. Inventors and software developers get 25 percent of the first $500,000, 20 percent of the second $500,000, and 15 percent thereafter of the royalties SRI receives.

The same policy applies in cases where SRI accepts stock in return for technology. I believe the policy has helped us retain good creative staff who might otherwise look elsewhere.

In conclusion, what I have outlined is by no means fixed. If there's one lesson we've learned it is that it's necessary to keep innovating if we are to continue finding new and different ways to get our technology into use. I'm very optimistic that the trends are favorable, for both contract research and technology commercialization. While the "NIH" factor is still very much alive, it has weakened. There's a greater receptivity by large corporations to outside ideas and technology.

There is also greater receptivity on the part of the newer and smaller corporations, who now come looking for that second and third product after they have experienced initial success. While these changes of attitude may only be temporary, it is my guess that, with continuing world technological competition, they are here to stay.

VI ENTREPRENEURIAL APPROACHES TO TECHNOLOGY COMMERCIALIZATION

14 TECHNOLOGY TRANSFER: ISSUES FOR CONSORTIA

John T. Pinkston

To incorporate advanced technology into new and improved products, two things are involved. First, the technology has to be created, and second, it must be delivered to the point of manufacturing. The second step has turned out to be at least as challenging as the first. This has come to be termed the "technology transfer" problem. Furthermore, we must address not only how we best incorporate advanced technology into new products and new services, but also how we do it in an expeditious way. The rapidity with which research results and know-how move from the laboratory to the production line will make the difference between maintaining a competitive advantage and losing technological leadership.

Let me define what I mean by *technology*. As I use the term, technology includes both the know-how by which significant value is added to a product and the tools that enable or facilitate the design and manufacture of a product.

For example, in the microelectronics field the integrated-circuit processing steps, or the process recipe, is clearly know-how. The fabrication equipment—the lithographic tools, the etchers, computer-aided design tools—are all tools that I include in my definition of technology. On this spectrum, there is a gray area—libraries of circuit device designs are clearly technology, but fall somewhere in between tools and know-how. Similarly, in the software area, development methodologies, structured programming, and object-oriented pro-gramming are know-how technology, and software tools such as lan-guage compilers and subroutine libraries are tool technology.

Some things may not be considered technology. I do not include advanced semiconductor devices or advanced materials as technology. Those are consumables. Technology is really the know-how, or some enduring capability for making or adding significant value to a product being produced.

The technology transfer problem is how to place these tools and know-how into operational use to carry out the process of adding value. Many different problems are involved in that process, and they call for different approaches.

I am told that in the Eskimo language there are many different words, each with a precise meaning, for what we simply call *snow*. They have snow that is hard, cold, and crystalline. They have snow that is warm and slushy. They have light snow and blowing snow. In English, we get along with using just one word. I would suggest that the term *technology transfer* is like our word *snow*. It may now be time to start considering that, like the Eskimos, we need to differentiate among the different concepts that are embodied in that term.

For example, one way that technology transfer problems vary is in the *willingness of the receiver* of the technology. This can range from highly motivated to downright hostile. In the latter case, the first task is selling and convincing before the actual technology transfer can begin.

Another dimension is the *motivation of the transmitter*, which can be willing, passive, or even resistant. The transfer can be from a willing transmitter — such as an internal R&D lab, a consortium like Micro-electronics and Computer Technology Corporation (MCC), or some university laboratories. Examples of a passive transmitter would be journal articles and literature. The resistant transmitter would be like a development engineer who honestly feels that his work isn't ready yet. Another example of a reluctant transmitter is a large company not wanting its technology to be used by competitors manufacturing plug-compatible products.

Third, problems differ fundamentally as a function of transfer *dis-tance*. The distance is short if the technology transfer is made within one group in one company. It gets a little bit longer if it occurs in the same company but from one group to another. It is still longer if you are going outside the company, or spanning large geographic distances. The shortest transfer distance occurs when the technology transfer is made within the same head—when the person who has worked on the technology development turns to the application.

MCC has recognized the need for reducing this generalized transfer distance by the way we have designed our structure. Research staff are assigned from the shareholder companies to come and participate side by side in the research. They can then go back to their companies, thereby shortening the distance over which this technology transfer has to take place.

A fourth dimension is the *form of the technology*. There is a spectrum from know-how on one end to tools on the other end, and there is a difference in the amount of learning that the receiver has to do across this spectrum. In general, it takes more learning and understanding to acquire the know-how than to learn to use a tool. This results in qualitatively different problems in getting the new technology into use. The challenge is one of encapsulation: the more a package can be encapsulated—the more the user only has to deal with the externals (as in the case of a tool)—the easier the technology transfer tends to be. The less encapsulated the package is, the more the user has to understand and master details of what is going on inside, and the more difficult it becomes.

A fifth dimension of technology transfer is how *radical* the new technology is. Is it an improvement on an already well understood and accepted process or technique? Or is it a complete change? For example, consider the movement to transistors from vacuum tubes. Substantial effort was required for tube technologists to master transistor technology and to understand its implications and be in a position to evaluate whether to take and use it. On the other hand, movement between semiconductor technologies, such as NMOS to CMOS, are much less radical (and less threatening).

Finally, a sixth variable is how the receiving organization intends to *acquire* the technology. There are many ways, and the techniques to enhance technology transfer depend on the method selected. A company can develop technology with its own R&D lab, but there are many other ways. A company can buy or license technology from others, paying royalties or exchanging patents. It can hire people who already have the know-how, or buy entire companies with the know-how. It can interact with research scientists in university laboratories, read the technical literature, or buy tools. A lot of technology transfer occurs simply with the purchase and installation of new tools or equipment. Yet another method of acquiring technology is by copying one's competitors. And last, but not least, a company can participate in consortia. Facilitating this incorporation of technology involves a range of activities across this spectrum of alternatives.

I can't leave this discussion of the variety of meanings that the term *technology transfer* has without relating an anecdote. Before I came to Austin, Texas, I worked for the federal government at an agency that is a member of the intelligence community. I worked for several years as my agency's representative to an interagency committee — under the director of Central Intelligence which was known as the Scientific and Technical Intelligence Committee. I can remember many meetings of this committee at which the topic of technology transfer was addressed. Do you think that the talk was concerned with how to facilitate this? Absolutely not! It was concerned with finding out how technology transfer is happening and putting a stop to it. We were, of course, talking about the undesired transfer of technology from Western nations to the Soviet bloc. Then I came to MCC and immediately entered into discussions of how to encourage technology transfer with our shareholder companies. I understood the difference, but it felt strange for a while to be using the same term *technology* transfer in that turned-around way.

Having seen the variety of forms that the technology transfer process can take, let me focus now on the problems that are faced by a consortium such as MCC. MCC was formed as a research consortium, owned by about nineteen U.S. high-tech companies. It was set up to do long-range, fundamental, high-payoff, high-risk research in the areas of electronics and computer technology. Presently, there are five research programs, each of whose costs and research results are shared by a set of the shareholder companies. Each of these research programs has evolved in its own way and has its own unique character, culture, and mission.

One can make some generalizations about MCC's problems with respect to each of these dimensions of the technology transfer problem space: the receiver's motivation, the transmitter's willingness, the transfer "distance," the form of the technology, the degree of novelty, and so on. As you would expect, the transmitter is uniformly willing and motivated. We very much want the results to move out to the shareholders. That will be a measure of our success. However, the receivers vary greatly. We are just now beginning to see a significant flow of results coming out of our pipeline as spinoffs occur from these research projects. Some of the shareholder companies are turning out to be clearly more aggressive in reaching in to take these results than others. This is a management difference among these companies. We see that there are also significant variations among the technical people within companies, as well as between companies themselves as to the degree of their receptiveness, their estimate of their readiness for the technology results, and the fit of the results to the company problem.

From observations so far, I have concluded that in a large number of cases the first task with the intended receiver is going to have to be salesmanship on our part before the job of communicating the technology details can really begin.

As an aside, I would offer an unsolved problem. Should a consortium like MCC carry out this job by working with the corporate research labs in the shareholder companies, or should it try to carry it out by working directly with the development people in the product development organizations? Neither way is perfect. Some of our companies clearly want us to operate in one way, while some want us to operate in the other. We are going to be getting experience with both of these methods, and each has its distinct advantages and disadvantages. The research lab adds another step in the chain, but tends to understand well the nature of the research process and results. The product-oriented people tend to be much more near-term in their perspective and less interested in long-term research results, but are closer to the real applications. How does one reach a balance? Before you say, "That is easy, just do it all," remember that this is a resource constrained problem.

With respect to the distance of technology transfer from the consortium to its members, it is relatively large. The technology transfer has to cross company boundaries, cultural boundaries, and large geographic distances. Furthermore, it is not as simple for us as a simple transfer from Culture A to Culture B. It is a transfer from Culture A to Cultures B, C, D, and F. Each one of them is distinct and different. Having worked for the government before coming to MCC, I would not have believed how diverse corporate cultures can be. That was one part of my education when I arrived. Companies are very different, and each of the transfers is going to have to be tailored to individual needs and ways of operating.

The form of the technology at MCC tends to be toward the know-how end of the spectrum. Some tools are going to be developed that will be more encapsulated. Even those are not likely to be purely turnkey. It is probable that we are going to be facing the more difficult end of that dimension — that we are going to have to transfer the less encapsulated kind of know-how technological results.

Finally, by the nature of our mission, the results tend to be fairly radical. This is going to add greatly to the challenge of preparing the receivers.

While this characterization of the space of technology transfer problems has allowed us to focus on the subspace that will require our attention, there is still a range of situations that we are going to be facing, with each calling for its own particular approach.

One thing comes through clearly. In addressing our problems, I keep coming back to focusing on the receiver. It takes two parties to effect a technology transfer — the transmitter and the receiver. Of these, the receiver is by far the more important. Transmitter motivation and willingness help, but the receiver *must* have motivation — in the form of either an excitement about new opportunities or a need to adopt new technology because there is no alternative in sight.

An example of the success that can occur when you have this enthusiasm is in the recent announcement from NCR of the first product that has reached the marketplace based primarily upon MCC technology. In the summer of 1987, an announcement was made in New York City about a software package call the Design Advisor, which NCR is offering to customers in their applications-specific integrated-circuit business. They had a very motivated young engineer who saw an opportunity for a package that MCC was developing to be incorporated into a product of the kind that she was working on. She came to MCC and spent about one week every month for a period of about one year. She was motivated by a clear concept in her own mind of a product. That was definitely technology pull. She came down and interacted with the researchers and grabbed hold of it and dragged it out. It worked, and it worked very well. As a result, NCR now has a product.

Characterizing a specific technology transfer problem according to where it falls along the dimensions that I have discussed will help to identify the barriers that need to be addressed, and actions to take to address them. If it is long distances, then you need to put in place the efforts to match cultures and provide communications. If it is radical and threatening technology, then you have to work on reassuring the receivers. If it is know-how that requires a deep background to absorb, you need to work hard on the education and training.

My conclusion is that the concept of a research consortium is sound. It provides important economies, through energy and risk-sharing for the participating companies and through mutual encouragement for its members. But it does not do it all. It cannot cause the incorporation of new technology into these companies. The receiver is still the key.

15 CREATING A UNIVERSITY TECHNOLOGY LICENSING OFFICE

Robert F. Gavin

The University of Michigan's technology licensing office, known as the Intellectual Properties Office, has undergone considerable change and growth in the past four years. Since each university's environment and culture is different, each university must develop its own style of technology transfer. Such things as the reporting structure of the university's technology transfer (licensing) office, and whether the office is viewed by the university primarily as a service for faculty or as a potential source of income for the university, may be functions of the university's tradition or history. However, this caveat being made, I would suggest that there are operational elements in any successful university's intellectual properties and technology transfer program that can be used by other universities interested in technology licensing.

A short history of the University of Michigan's technology licensing program shows that until 1981 the University allocated few resources toward intellectual properties. In mid-1981 the University hired an attorney to act as a full-time patent administrator. In 1982 the University hired a second attorney, and I filled that position. By 1985 the activities of the office had increased, and we hired one additional attorney and a marketing representative. I proposed creation of the marketing representative position to change the focus of our technology licensing efforts from being strictly legal to being a combination of marketing, business, and legal functions. I felt that universities had not

151

emphasized marketing their technologies. So we began a new program of marketing, emphasizing development of corporate contacts. Our first marketing representative had received an M.B.A. from the University of Michigan and was previously involved in technical sales. Thus, in 1985, the office consisted of three lawyers, a marketing representative, an administrative assistant, and two support staff.

I am the Director of the Intellectual Properties Office and Intellectual Property Counsel and report to the Vice President for Research. There are two full-time marketing representatives as well as Associate and Assistant Intellectual Property Counsels, and an Administrative Associate who manages the affairs of the office. As part of the office we also have a recently opened incubation facility with a part-time manager. Finally, we have created several summer internship positions for marketing associates from the University's M.B.A. program.

Any university wishing to develop its technology licensing operations should sit down and develop its own plan. In developing the University of Michigan's business plan, we first identified the objectives that had become important to the University of Michigan and created a strategy to meet those objectives. This relatively simple process is important to any university wanting to increase the effectiveness of its technology licensing operation. The objectives should be listed in their order of importance to the university—we put service to the University research community first on the list. Second is delivery of the results of University research to the private sector. Assistance in increasing the technology base of local business is third, and generation of revenue and business opportunities for the researchers and the University is last.

Service is a key word in having a successful operation. If a technology transfer operation serves our first two objectives—service to the research community, and delivery of results to the stream of commerce—the last two objectives will almost automatically be met.

While saying this, I would also point out that any technology licensing operation should function as a profit center for the university. If an operation is to have a long-term history and survive through thick and thin and the university budget process, it must become a profit center for the university.

The third goal for the University of Michigan is assistance with increasing the competitive abilities and technology base of local business. There are those who would disagree with this objective. However, I suggest that such an objective is appropriate for a state university, particularly a university in a state such as Michigan, which has experienced some economic difficulty.

One indicator of the Intellectual Properties Office's fulfillment of the first objective of service to the University research community is that the University research community's use of the office's services has increased over 300 percent in the last several years. In 1984 we were receiving thirty invention disclosures per year, and by fiscal 1987 we received close to ninety disclosures from University researchers. One reason we are able to draw this increased attention from researchers is that the research community feels the office performs a valuable service.

Achievement of the second objective of the University's technology licensing program — delivery of results of University research to the private sector — can be measured by looking at such factors as patent applications filed during a given year, patents issued during that year, and the total number of patents pending during each year. In 1982 the University of Michigan had only two patents pending and expended $120 million in sponsored research funding. By fiscal 1984 we had $180 million in sponsored research funding. By 1984 we had over twenty patents pending; in that year, we filed thirteen applications. In fiscal 1986 we filed thirteen patent applications and had nine new patents with $180 million in sponsored research funding. In 1987 we had only

Figure 15–1.   University of Michigan Intellectual Properties.

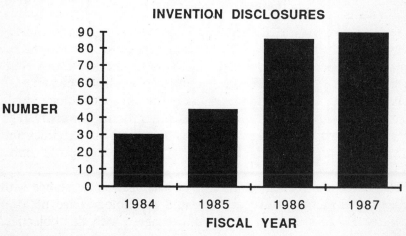

two patents issued, yet the number of patents filed in 1987, i.e., twenty-five, represents a significant increase over previous years. By fiscal year-end in 1987, we had over fifty-three patents pending. Finally, in the eleven-month period between July 1, 1987, and June 1, 1988, twelve patents have been issued to the University of Michigan; this is representative of a continuing upward trend.

The number of patents pending is not equivalent to the delivery of research results to the commercial sector, but it is a clear indicator of intentions and opportunities for commercialization. A more tangible measure of success may be licensing agreements; we have closed a number of these and now have over twenty technologies that are producing revenues for the University. Due to the time lag between filing a patent application and its issuance, a university should assume that its patent licensing program will take three to seven years of investment before developing significant results.

One reason that patent activity is an indicator of success is that it is much easier to license a patent or patent application than it is to license what I call "raw technology" (nonproprietary technology). Also, in a university setting, once researchers identify an interesting

Figure 15–2.   Delivery of Results of Research, University of Michigan.

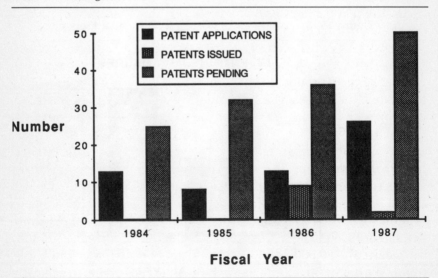

discovery or invention, they are hard pressed not to publish; publishing is an important and integral part of the university culture. If the university is not aggressive about filing for patents, this tendency in the university environment to publish quickly will eliminate the possibility for a long-term patent-licensing program and lead to the frustration of many creative faculty wishing to see their research developed into socially useful products and processes.

Fulfillment of the third University objective, i.e., increasing the technology base of local business, requires that we take an active interest in local business. We work to create new businesses that utilize university technology through licensing, and we also provide assistance to established businesses by licensing inventions for expansion and improvement of the businesses' existing product lines.

In the first area, we work with University researchers and inventors to assist them in looking at the appropriateness of the federal government's Small Business Innovative Research (SBIR) grants and contracts programs. We help entrepreneurially inclined faculty through the incubation facility, which is part of our office. With the incubation facility, we are able to work with faculty who might otherwise be unable to start a business or gain access to the grants of the SBIR program. We have found the SBIR program to be a success, although the $50,000 cap on Phase I funding can be a difficult limitation, and without bridge financing, the hiatus between Phase I and Phase II SBIR funding can seriously undermine a small company's product development efforts.

In working with existing local companies, we have licensed University-developed technology to such companies as a means of enhancing their product lines. As part of this effort we have assisted local small businesses with submissions of their SBIR grants in conjunction with licensing transactions between the companies and the University.

In reviewing the final technology transfer objective for the Intellectual Properties Office, i.e., generation of revenue for the University and its researchers, we see that gross royalty revenues for the University of Michigan have been rising in a fairly steady and dramatic fashion. In 1982 we received a little over $200,000 in annual royalties and in 1984 the figure rose to $500,000 in annual royalties. In 1987 we received $750,000 in royalties, and this represents a continuing trend. We are quite bullish about the University's ability to achieve a significant revenue stream as a result of the technology licensing program. When looking at the number and kinds of agreements we have executed, and under which products are being developed by companies, we anticipate that the University will experience a significant increase in royalty revenues over the next three years—perhaps $2 million per year in royalties within three years.

What are our office's basic strategies for achieving the objectives that are appropriate to the University of Michigan? First is small-business development. The Intellectual Properties Office works with existing small businesses and with University researchers wishing to start their own companies. This strategy has resulted in the formation of five businesses utilizing University technologies. Of these, two have demonstrated the potential for staying power: one is a biotech company, and the other is in pharmaceuticals. As these companies and other similar companies expand, it is possible that they will become a "farm system" for development of University technologies.

Corporate networking is another function and strategy for a technology transfer office. Networking provides a source of expert advice on a variety of technology and market areas and gives an immediate source of licensing potential. Long-term relationships between the university and industry result in increased corporate interest, both in funding university research and in licensing, developing, and

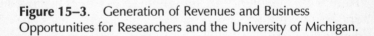

Figure 15–3.   Generation of Revenues and Business Opportunities for Researchers and the University of Michigan.

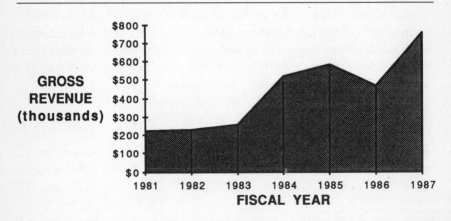

commercializing its results. Corporate networking is an absolutely vital element in our strategy for technology transfer; we have over 700 corporate contacts on our active mailing lists. An office newsletter is very helpful in keeping up with companies, and we also distribute a booklet listing the technologies available for licensing.

Finally, we found the University's M.B.A. program to be a good source of corporate networking. We began employing work-study students from the M.B.A. program in 1985. In addition to gathering marketing analysis information, these students will become long-term sources of information for our office and, potentially, will become corporate contacts themselves.

With respect to timing and finance, software is perhaps the only university-generated intellectual property or technology that has an immediate commercial potential. This is contrasted to patented technologies that we have the ability to "work the technology" — to market it, to license it, and to encourage companies to develop products using it — all paying off in three to seven years. The revenues generated from patents are likely to be more significant than those generated from software, however the potential for revenue from software is immediate. Our ability to market and license software is important in creating cash flow to justify the University's short-term investment to achieve its long-term goals for a technology licensing office. We have six software programs that we market directly to end-users.

To sum up, the following concepts should be kept in mind if you are interested in working with a university technology licensing office, or in developing one. First is service to the university research community. Another is the profit-center concept. Developing a combination of marketing/business/legal expertise is also important. Licensing to both small companies and large corporations is important because of the broad spectrum of technology that can be licensed from a university research base. Software can be a cash flow generator. And, finally, effective marketing is a key to overall success.

16 THE FEDERAL LABORATORIES: EFFECTIVE PARTNERS IN INNOVATION DEVELOPMENT

Eugene E. Stark, Jr.

Federal labs are effective partners in technology commercialization because they represent major technology resources. They present valuable opportunities for the growing variety of methods by which industry and others work with federal laboratories. A Federal Laboratory Consortium network eases the issue of access to federal labs and also provides a glimpse of a future that we might hope to see.

In terms of the resources of the federal laboratories, many are surprised to know the number, the size, and the variety of things that the labs do. The United States has over 100 "major" laboratories — those having in-house R&D budgets of at least $20 million. They employ about 100,000 professional scientists and engineers, who constitute about one-sixth of our nation's total supply of scientists and engineers. They perform about $20 billion per year of in-house research, development, testing, and evaluation, only a small fraction of which is directly classified. These laboratories work in virtually every area in science and technology — from obvious areas such as agriculture and electronics to those that one might not expect, such as biotechnology, genetic engineering, and instrumentation development.

There are tangible resources at the laboratories. The laboratories have a wide variety of facilities and equipment — many of which cannot be found elsewhere — that are, in fact, rapidly available to university researchers and industry researchers. In some cases, these facilities and equipment are there solely for the use of users from outside the

159

laboratory. In other cases, they are available on an "as available" basis for research. An important step, for example, has been the Department of Energy's allowing industry to use these facilities in a proprietary way in order to own the results of that work. That is a major step for economic development and commercialization.

There is a remarkable base of expertise within the laboratories. Laboratories are buildings and equipment, but they are also people who have the technological expertise to be transferred to industry. These laboratories generate a wide variety of innovations.

To many people, innovations mean patents. Based upon history, many innovations have not been patented. One reason is that government tries very hard to protect itself against paying inflated prices or royalties for products that were originally developed at government expense. Another reason is that people in federal laboratories have not had an incentive to even consider the patentability of their inventions. In fact, strong disincentives have existed — such as going through a barrage of paperwork and having to deal with lawyers. Why should one do that when nothing will pay off? As I note later, that attitude is changing quite rapidly.

A number of mission programs in federal laboratories have direct application in the commercial marketplace. There are major programs by the Agricultural Research Service and the U.S. Forest Service that feed directly into industry. The Agricultural Research Service is foremost among the federal agencies in writing cooperative agreements with industry. There are also spin-off opportunities. Under these agreements, technology has been developed for defense and for future large-scale energy programs. These technologies can have other immediate applications, such as support software or instrumentation. Another program, the effects of which we are just beginning to see, is the federal government's response to recent advances in superconductivity. A number of Department of Energy laboratories have creative flexibility, with superconductivity budgets in excess of $10 million per year per laboratory.

Laboratories now have a strong positive policy to cooperate with industry. When technology transfer was only a buzzword in the 1960s, NASA seemed to be doing something that really worked. In the 1970s, technology transfer turned into something that laboratories outside of NASA began to talk about. Now in the 1980s, and into the future, technology transfer will be a bona fide requirement, and a genuine core mission, of all federal laboratories.

The Stevenson-Wydler Act of 1980, amended in the Technology Transfer Act of 1986, for the first time gave a clear congressional mandate that all federal laboratories have, in the President's words, an "open-door" policy and a clear mission for technology transfer. Now part of the job responsibility of every scientist and engineer in a federal laboratory is to consider potential spin-offs from their work. The law also allowed direct licensing of patents by federal agencies. In many cases, federal laboratories would be guaranteed a 15 percent royalty share.

The new law allows laboratories to enter into cooperative agreements with industry. Labs can write agreements with industry that specify in advance the distribution of intellectual property, know-how, patents, and copyrights that result from cooperative efforts.

A 1987 presidential order essentially said that the President expected the agencies to implement the act rather rapidly. When Congress passes an act, that doesn't mean that anything is necessarily going to happen. It takes an interest by the administration to make something happen — the President made his interest clear in an executive order.

Increasingly, we see strong pushes not only from Washington but also from industry. Until recently, some companies didn't really want to deal with the federal labs. But now they have new corporate policies reflecting changes in their needs and changes in the government's attitude. They want to take advantage of federal laboratory technology, and thus a strong policy for cooperation is developing.

Internal laboratory motivation strengthens this process. A share of individual investors' patent royalties is allocated to the laboratories themselves, and labs can put that money into discretionary research. Aside from the few such laboratories at the Department of Energy, most federal laboratories have no funds for discretionary research, and the new policy is quite an incentive for them.

One can reasonably question the very existence of some number of federal laboratories around the country. Haven't they fulfilled their mission? Shouldn't they be closed? Is there really a future role for federal labs? Shouldn't this government R&D money perhaps go directly to industry so that the results of the R&D are, by definition, already transferred to industry? Those are questions that are tough to answer, but enhanced institutional respect is a key element to strengthening the laboratories' very existence. The ability to work collaboratively with universities and industries is important. Technology inflow enhances institutional respect and understanding and is important for the future of the federal laboratories.

A variety of modes of cooperation exists between federal labs and both industry and universities; federal laboratory researchers can go to industry and industry people can come to the laboratories. Many have been able to work it out so that there is full protection and reciprocity on intellectual properties. If a laboratory person is loaned to industry, he is not supposed to bring back any information that is proprietary. Not only that, but anything that he develops while he is at the company remains proprietary to the company. That is something quite new.

We have some similar joint programs where federal labs work with each other as well as with industry. Whether we are exchanging money, or whether we are both working under government funds, or whether we are simply working together and collaborating because we see some commonality of goals in our research programs, we work together. Licensing of intellectual property is often seen as a wonderful treat, where one exchanges financial payment for some information and expertise. That is a far more cooperative phenomenon than many might expect.

Entrepreneurship is a growing method of technology commercialization from federal laboratories. We are beginning to see a long stream of spin-offs in the form of new companies. Perhaps we will start mentioning the fact that Lincoln Lab, under some definition, is a federal laboratory; we could take credit for Digital Equipment Corporation in that way. We are also seeing a number of small business spin-offs from federal laboratories in the last few years.

Finally, perhaps the most important point is the critical payoffs that come from collaboration at the person-to-person level. There can be institutional cooperation and programmatic cooperation, but by the time all is said and done, these types of cooperation work only if people cooperate with people. This cooperation must occur at the scientific and engineering level, and at the managerial level as well.

I will give just a few examples of existing cooperation with industry.

The Oak Ridge National Laboratory (ORNL), a little over a year ago, decided to instigate the formation of an industry consortium to support the development of advanced ceramics. There now exists the Ceramics Advancement Manufacturing, Development, and Engineering Center (CAMDEC). Because ORNL established it outside its own laboratory, CAMDEC has suddenly become interested in where it can find technology and has developed a relationship with the National Bureau of Standards. Several companies have signed up for CAMDEC, which requires a multiyear commitment of something in excess of $50,000.

The Maryland Biotechnology Consortium brings together the National Bureau of Standards, Maryland's Montgomery County, and the University of Maryland. They are sharing the National Bureau of Standard's buildings and equipment resources. The county and the university are providing funding and people to work together on biotechnology development.

The Synchroton Light Source at Brookhaven National Laboratory is a national user facility funded by the Department of Energy. Brookhaven is beginning to find some rather strong industrial interest in duplicating its actual light source technology on a smaller scale for X-ray lithography photography in the semiconductor industry. At Los Alamos, researchers are using a DNA sequence database in cooperation with a firm in the Boston area, attempting to put in one place all of the information that is coming out of the genetic research area so that people don't waste resources or spend time finding sequences that already exist.

The National Bureau of Standards has a well-known set of research associates programs. The National Bureau of Standard's facility serves as the basic research facility for the nation's dental industry because the dental supply companies send people to do research there. When the industrial researchers reach a point where they see product possibilities, they go back to their own companies to complete their research on a proprietary basis.

Finally, in a large number of laboratories we see programs sponsored by start-up companies or very large corporations that would like to sponsor research and development within federal laboratories based upon the special expertise of those laboratories.

In genetic engineering, everything is occurring, from state-of-the-art research to the development of new agricultural products, such as grains that can be grown in southern New Mexico in saline soil in arid conditions. Materials technology is an area that cuts across many federal laboratories because of the needs of the weapons complex, whether conventional or nuclear, as well as the special needs of high-temperature and corrosive environments and energy programs. Medical diagnostics turns out to be partly an objective and partly a spin-off of the activities of federal laboratories.

Manufacturing technology is one important thrust of the federal government within the Department of Defense, the National Bureau of Standards, NASA, and the Department of Energy. The Federal Laboratory Consortium was recently approached by an industrial research institute and asked whether there was some way that we could help industry understand what the government was doing in manufacturing technology. As it turned out, even some DOD contractors who were doing work for the DOD's manufacturing and technology program did not know the full scope or the full scale of opportunities. So we sponsored a conference at the Wright Patterson Air Force Base in Ohio in March of 1988 to make that information available to American industry.

Another area is instrumentation. There has been a lot of work on superconductivity. It may be surprising, but building technology is something that is important to this country. The National Research Council and the Building Research Board have asked the federal labs to work with them to define state-of-the-art technology to develop the nation's building industry.

Entrepreneurship is growing rapidly. We see fluidics technology coming out of the army's Harry Diamond Laboratory, giving rise not only to the formation of a small company in Maryland but to Garrett Airline Services in Arizona. There is an electronic identification company, which was in Los Alamos, New Mexico, until very recently. They have become so successful that they outgrew local facilities and moved to Santa Fe, with second-round venture capital financing that came from Texas.

Accelerators are abstruse instruments to many. The Meson Physics Facility accelerator developed in Los Alamos and completed about fifteen years ago, led to a technology spin-off that is now the basis for the generation of all medical x-rays in the world today. There were other spin-offs for production-related and other applications in the medical field. Sandia Laboratory at Livermore, California, has recently allowed one of its employees to leave with an air-treatment technology that removes the oxides of nitrogen and cleans up the air.

Oversensitive diagnostics is an area that has seen several spin-offs, including a group called Atom Sciences from the Oak Ridge National Laboratory. These are just a few examples. I would like to point out that there are other programs—which are either instigated by or collaborative efforts with federal laboratories—that have made major contributions. The IC^2 Institute, through a number of conferences and suggestions, has had a major influence on incubators associated with federal laboratories and on federal laboratory programs. The Ohio Technology Transfer Organization is a group of community colleges in Ohio that networks to deliver solutions to problems, as well as technologies, to small businesses in Ohio. There is the Institute for Technology Development in the state of Mississippi. The High Technology Council is working with the universities and is beginning to work with federal laboratories to make federal laboratory technology available to industries in Florida. A mayor's task force is drawing heavily on the Argonne National Lab and the Fermi National Accelerator Laboratory in the Chicago area and is tying them in with industry based in the Chicago area. The Washington Advanced Research Foundation is again trying to work with a number of universities and their intellectual properties to make sure that intellectual property is well utilized. Very recently, city and industry leaders in the greater Baltimore area are beginning to work with a large number of federal laboratories in the Maryland and Virginia area to look for technology-based development opportunities.

I would like to describe to you our national network of federal laboratories called the Federal Laboratory Consortium. We have as members over 400 laboratories and centers around the country, from about eleven different federal agencies. We have just established, as required by the Technology Transfer Act, a national referral clearinghouse, which is so far a one-man PC database operation in San Diego.

The key point of the Federal Laboratory Consortium is not to be bureaucratic, but to keep the potential linkages between businesses and laboratories out in the field. Therefore, we stress regional operations and have divided the country up into six geographic regions. We provide a network of individuals throughout those federal labs who can provide access and referral. The major support services of our Federal Laboratory Consortium include an efficient network and clearinghouse. When someone from industry has a particular technology-based interest — whether it be a problem or a search for a specific type of technology — by contacting one of our regional coordinators or the individual at our clearinghouse in San Diego, we will find whatever resource we can, if it exists. The right person in the right laboratory, wherever he or she may be in the country, will talk with the interested person about that technology. These are not reports, not referrals, not committees, but an individual with whom he or she may deal at a working level. We work internally to develop and transfer newfound methods of technology transfer among the federal laboratories. We address barriers and take some national initiatives.

From a broad standpoint, we feel that federal laboratory cooperation is a major opportunity for all segments of American business. For small businesses, it is an opportunity to obtain free assistance from our people, to obtain technology from the laboratories, and to use entrepreneurship and spin-offs from our laboratories as a basis for new businesses. For industry, it is a source of innovation and an opportunity for staff development, for both government and industry researchers and engineers. We see growing opportunities for interaction with universities in the research area, as well as with state and local governments, which after all are major components of our economy and major sources of services whose productivity is very important in our overall economy.

Finally, I would like to mention a few thoughts about my vision of the future. I am not sure how far into the future this vision is. The optimist in me says five years, and the pessimist in me says maybe fifteen years. First of all, "precompetitive" collaboration will be routine — that is, the collaboration, we hope, of most companies with federal laboratories at a stage before they are really competing with other companies in their industry, following somewhat the model that we see in Japan. (Perhaps MCC is the model for this.) We hope to see laboratories engaging in short-term and long-term relationships with businesses of all sizes. Many interactions over the past years have been fairly ad hoc and fairly well focused on a single piece of technology. Among the things that we really like to see are long-term relationships.

We would like to see, sometime in the future, a significant number of the technical staff in our federal laboratories working there on assignment from industry and from universities. This is carried on routinely in Japan, where in their government research institutes, as I understand it, between 30 and 50 percent of the people at any one time are not government employees but employees of industries or universities. That is the way to keep the network going, to keep exciting innovation developing, and most importantly, to maintain the links among institutions.

Cooperation should be strong at both the technical and management levels. There are numerous examples of good cooperation at the management level that never quite seem to fit the troops, as well as examples of good cooperation at the technical level, despite, rather than because of, management's efforts. I would surely like to see both sets working together. Perhaps most importantly of all, we see cooperative research development in innovation emphasizing the strategic view of future possibilities. That is a view of five or ten more years down the line, rather than of the next quarter's profit-and-loss statement, coupled with a healthy acceptance of risk. This is aimed not at industry but at the federal laboratories, because we tell ourselves and tell the world that our role is to do the long-range, risky R&D that perhaps industry does not want to fund.

In summary, the federal laboratories really are effective partners and can be more effective partners. The key to it is individual interest on person-to-person, company-to-company, and company-to-laboratory levels. We will never have a national model that simply says, "Company, if you would like to work with federal labs, just plug yourself in this way." It really is an institution-to-institution and case-by-case situation in which we can all learn from one another and can forge better institutional relationships. There is just not a national model. There is no computer program that tells us how to choose a spouse or how to make a marriage work. Laboratory-industry interaction can be no simpler than that.

VII SUMMARY AND CONCLUSIONS

17 TOMORROW'S TRANSFORMATIONAL MANAGERS

George Kozmetsky

The structure of this book reflects, in many respects, a definite break from the traditional approach to entrepreneurship. It has served to provide a better understanding so as to develop and improve the present state of managerial art and practice across the spectrum of emerging industries.

Emerging industries are those that will be developed by using revolutionary technologies that are only now beginning to move from invention to innovation, such as new materials, biotechnology, and telecommunications. These will be the key new industries for global competition and cooperation. Around these industries will develop economic growth, job creation, and new business developments. Around these industries will develop newer centers of innovation and manufacturing. Emerging industries are the drivers for determining a new approach to management, if we are to maintain preeminence scientifically and economically. Entrepreneurial managers must be more creative and innovative than today's traditional professional managers or today's entrepreneurs.

These emerging industries have the following four characteristics:

1. They are so encompassing that no one country can dominate them completely.
2. They are linked to areas of basic sciences that are also undergoing revolutionary changes.

171

3. They are immediately transferable to rapidly industrializing nations.
4. They are key to leap-frogging for basic industries.

Emerging industries are being challenged across all dimensions, from scientific development to invention, to innovation, to commercialization. Consequently, entrepreneurial managers must deal with academia and government in new ways to help meet the scientific challenges involved in commercializing emerging technologies through successful, globally competitive companies.

This volume identifies the need to blend the best elements of entrepreneurship with professional management. The traditional belief has been that entrepreneurs cannot manage; they can initiate and bring a firm to take-off, but eventually they must step aside for professional managers during the business's organizational — or the corporation's mature growth — stage. There has emerged a newer recognition that today's professional management must move to a more entrepreneurial approach and style focused on developing new-to-the-world products, new markets, and new modes of operations.

To date, it is no exaggeration to point out that the study and practice of entrepreneurship on the one hand and traditional professional management on the other have been largely separated and segmented. It has been as though the concepts were distinct and entirely different. Some key work has begun to show that these two streams of study and practice are converging, especially through a focus on intrapreneurship.

Intrapreneurship is based on the same principles as entrepreneurship. They both require the fusion of talent, ideas, capital, and know-how. The term *entrepreneurship* is generally used to designate individuals starting their own businesses. The term *intrapreneurship* is usually used to refer to entrepreneurship within large corporations. As entrepreneurial firms grow, they generally find the need for more traditional management expertise and disciplines. Too often, as at Apple, they push the entrepreneur out. By the same token, as many mature firms with excellent traditional management grow, they find the need for more intrapreneurship. That's when the leveraged buy-out (LBO) and mergers-and-acquisitions (M&A) entrepreneur comes in. The combination of entrepreneurial and intrapreneurial management is what Peter Drucker has called "entrepreneurial management."

This volume has focused on what both large and small corporations need to learn about entrepreneurial management—and on why they need to do it—from the point of view of being creative and innovative within our existing businesses, as well as within emerging firms.

Intrapreneurs are advocates of innovation within the corporation, but they do not necessarily assume the financial risk of the business. Intrapreneurs are viewed as champions of a product, or as executive mentors who have direct or indirect influence over the resource allocation process and who use their power to channel resources to newer innovations. Intrapreneurial characteristics are:

- extraordinary involvement with new ideas;
- possessing energy to cope with indifference and resistance;
- displaying persistence, commitment, and dedication; and
- courage of heroic dimensions.

Rosabeth Moss Kanter has labeled intrapreneurs as "change masters." She defines them as "people who envision something and make it work. They don't start businesses; they improve them."[1] I believe that intrapreneurial management is more challenging and fun than being a traditional manager by the books, which our M.B.A. programs emphasize.

Let me sum up some of the key points made in the chapters of this book in terms of management.

THE CHARACTERISTICS OF SUCCESSFUL ENTREPRENEURIAL MANAGERS

I. Personal Skills
  A. Style of thinking: creating a shared vision of a realistic, credible, and attractive future for the betterment of the organization
  B. Operating on emotional and spiritual resources, in contrast to more traditional managerial allocation of physical resources
  C. Having a synthesized vision that encompasses:
    1. Foresight—how the vision fits the organization environment
    2. Hindsight—does not violate policies, tradition, and culture
    3. Global view—world competitive view

    4.   Depth perception — sees appropriate responses from competitors

    5.   Peripheral vision — understands responses from competitors

    6.   Revision — can change as the innovation progresses over a long period of time

D. Communication and articulation abilities

E. Persistence

F. Trust

G. Ability to keep up-to-date and to keep learning

II. Interpersonal Skills

    A. Builds coalitions between people and:

        1. Funds

        2. Information sources

        3. Champions

        4. High levels of management support

    B. Understands the process of innovation and change for the organization; for example, is skilled at:

        1. Seed-planting

        2. Tin-cupping

        3. Horse-trading

        4. Sanity-checking

        5. Building and working through teams

        6. Sharing credit

Entrepreneurial management within the corporation involves dealing with creativity and innovation. Table 17–1 helps to differentiate between management and managers. Creative management is what managers of research and development organizations, as well as sole entrepreneurs, deal with — namely, new things. Innovative management is what entrepreneurs must do especially in the start-up phase, and what traditional professional managers deal with in the take-off phase, particularly in marketing, production, and finance. Creative and innovative management is the province of the leadership of organizations and of entrepreneurial managers.

Entrepreneurial management is grounded in the belief that leadership makes a significant difference in the way organizations respond to and cope with change, especially those that are dependent on new technology and market development. Such management is deeply

Table 17–1. Construct for Creative and Innovative Management.

Construct	Key Elements/Knowledge Blocks
Creative Management	New Idea
	New Directions
	New Concepts
	New Methods
	New Modes of Operation
Innovative Management	Ability to implement successfully
	Ability to move successfully in new directions

involved with creating real economic value and with adapting personal aspirations to the evolving objectives of the firm as well as to the larger goals of the American society. In this context, technology is the driver. Over the next decade, technology will be increasingly viewed as a national and world resource, as a generator of wealth, as a means to increase productivity and international trade, as an area for assessment of private and public risk-taking, and as a key factor in improving the organization, education, and training of entrepreneurial managers and the work force.

Entrepreneurial and traditional managers in large corporations do not always fit comfortably together. A very dramatic example is the recent Roger Smith and Ross Perot confrontation at GM. There have been many instances with even more dramatic results. Some years ago at 3M, a researcher was fired. He kept coming back to the laboratory to work on his project, off the payroll. He persisted. He was successful. He was rehired. His project became a division. He retired as vice president of a very successful operation.

Entrepreneurial managers are keys to renewal in an organization. They are self-motivated and easy to spot. They are not easy to manage. Most traditional managers do not understand how they think and what they want. While entrepreneurial managers are visionaries, they ar not daydreamers. They are driven. They cross over boundaries and get into turf trouble. They are as politically oriented as they are technically oriented.

Entrepreneurial managers require situations that can challenge them with aggressive goals. They must have scientific and technological breakthroughs and new market needs to help them gain access to resources. They sometimes need to be bailed out when some of their programs inevitably falter. They need to be given the proper rewards; recognition is, in many respects, more important than the traditional monetary reward. They need to have career tracks, or they leave!

This book has focused on two critical components for entrepreneurial management: namely, linking technology with new market development. Why is linking innovation with new market development important? To survive, succeed, and flourish in a hypercompetitive world and market, it is important to deal with technological obsolescence; to diffuse new technology for multiple applications for new products and services; to handle short product life cycles and educate the marketplace, as well as regulatory agencies, about the worldwide possible locations for science and manufacturing functions; and to develop competitive trade policies if we are to do business in today's global marketplace. The way to deal with these issues in both a timely and effective way must be through entrepreneurial management.

NOTES

1. Rosabeth Moss Kanter, *The Change Masters: Innovation for Productivity in the American Corporation* (New York: Simon and Schuster, 1985).

INDEX

ABOUT THE EDITOR

Kenneth D. Walters is dean and professor of business administration at the School of Business, California Polytechnic State University, in San Luis Obispo, California.

Before he assumed his present position in 1983, he was chairman of the Department of Business, Government, and Society, in the Graduate School of Business Administration at the University of Washington in Seattle.

He has written numerous articles for the *Harvard Business Review*, the *California Management Review*, the *Columbia Journal of World Business*, *Ecology Law Quarterly*, and other leading journals. He coauthored (with R.J. Monsen) the book *Nationalized Companies*.

He has written and lectured widely on the increasing international competition facing U.S. business and on American strategies for commercializing scientific research and new technology.

A graduate of Stanford Law School in 1966, he also holds a Ph.D. in business administration from the University of California, Berkeley.

ABOUT THE CONTRIBUTORS

Michael L. Bandler is vice president of Network Engineering and planning for Pacific Bell. Mr. Bandler began his Bell System career in 1961. By 1975 he was appointed chief engineer for New York City. In 1981 he transferred to AT&T as a director in marketing, then assumed his present position with Pacific Bell in 1982. Mr. Bandler was also president of the California Engineering Foundation from 1985 to 1987. He received a B.E.E. degree from Cornell University, and his M.B.A. from New York University.

Herbert W. Boyer is cofounder of Genentech, Inc., founded in 1976. Genentech is the first company to commercialize products made with recombinant-DNA technology. Dr. Boyer is a professor of biochemistry and biophysics at the University of California, San Francisco. He has received many honors, including induction into the California Inventors Hall of Fame (1982) and the Industrial Research Institute's Distinguished Achievement Award in 1982. He was elected to the National Academy of Science in 1985. Dr. Boyer did his graduate study in bacteriology and microbial genetics at the University of Pittsburgh and Yale University.

E. Oran Brigham is chairman, chief executive officer, and president of Avantek, Inc. His background includes extensive experience with a wide range of electronics technologies, including telecommunications equipment, electronic defense and intelligence systems, and signal processing products. In 1986 Dr. Brigham was named a "gold-medal winner" by the *Wall Street Transcript*, recognizing him as "the best chief executive in the telecommunications equipment industry during 1985." A widely published author, his credits include several college-level textbooks. Dr. Brigham earned B.S.E.E. and M.S.E.E. degrees, as well as a Ph.D. in 1967, at the University of Texas, Austin.

G. Steven Burrill is the chairman of Arthur Young's National High Technology Group. Mr. Burrill directs and coordinates the firm's services to clients in biotechnology, computers, telecommunications, and related high-technology industries. He has personally assisted the start-up of more than 125 high-tech companies, lending his expertise to help them grow, find adequate capital, and solve accounting, tax, financial, and strategic matters. Mr. Burrill graduated from the University of Wisconsin, Madison, with a B.B.A. degree in accounting and finance in 1966.

Klaus Dahl is principal scientist for Raychem, the company he joined in 1967 as a staff scientist. Dr. Dahl has worked on the use of high-performance polymers in aircraft and spacecraft applications. He has also studied thermoplastic polymers, the development of adhesives, and the electrochemistry of corrosion protection systems. Dr. Dahl has researched electrically conductive ceramics and is now working on the use of optical materials for display purpose imaging. Born in Berlin, Dr. Dahl received a degree in chemical engineering at the state school before immigrating to Canada. He received his Ph.D. from McGill University in Montreal and later went to Munich University on a NATO Fellowship for postdoctoral study.

Robert F. Gavin is a member of the University of Michigan's Office of the General Counsel. Mr. Gavin's title is that of intellectual property counsel and director of the university's Intellectual Properties Office, which is responsible for the protection, marketing, and commercialization of university-owned technologies, including patents, copyrights, and trade secrets. Mr. Gavin received his J.D. from Wayne State University in 1980, and a B.A. degree in 1973 from the University of Michigan.

John J. Gilman is senior scientist for the Center for Advanced Materials at Lawrence Berkeley Laboratory. Dr. Gilman's career has combined teaching and industrial research. He taught at the Illinois Institute of Technology, Rensselaer Polytechnic Institute, Brown University, and the University of Illinois. His industrial research was done at the Crucible Steel Company of America and at the General Electric

Company. Dr. Gilman has published approximately 170 technical papers and six books and is a member of the National Academy of Engineering.

George Kozmetsky is director of the IC² Institute at the University of Texas, Austin. In addition, Dr. Kozmetsky is executive associate for economic affairs of the University of Texas System and a professor of management and computer science at UT-Austin. Until 1982, Dr. Kozmetsky served as dean of the College of Business Administration and the Graduate School of Business. Dr. Kozmetsky is cofounder, a director, and former executive vice president of Teledyne, Inc. He is an acknowledged expert in high technology and venture capital, providing special testimony on business and technology issues to state and federal legislators. Two of his recent books are *Transformational Management* and *Financing and Managing Fast Growth Companies: The Venture Capital Process*. Dr. Kozmetsky holds advanced degrees from the University of Washington and Harvard University.

Alvin L. Kwiram is vice provost and professor of chemistry at the University of Washington in Seattle. Prior to his present position, he served as chairman of the Department of Chemistry at the University of Washington, where he was instrumental in founding the Center for Process Analytical Chemistry. Dr. Kwiram holds a doctorate from the California Institute of Technology and is internationally known for his scholarly contributions on the determination of molecular structure and the development of new technology and instrumentation for this purpose.

Richard A. Marciano is vice president for technology commercialization and assistant to the president at SRI International. Mr. Marciano provides general staff support to SRI's president and CEO, with particular emphasis on managing issues and policy development with institutewide implications. As director and chief operating officer for technology commercialization of the SRI Development Company, Mr. Marciano is responsible for SRI's technology commercialization interests. Mr. Marciano studied engineering at Brown University and received his B.A. degree from Syracuse University.

John T. Pinkston is vice president and chief scientist at Microelectronics and Computer Technology Corporation (MCC). He is responsible for establishing MCC's technical agenda and for providing technical consultation and oversight for MCC's research programs. Prior to joining MCC, Dr. Pinkston served with the National Security Agency

(NSA) for sixteen years. He held various positions in research managment at NSA. Immediately prior to joining MCC, he was serving as deputy chief of NSA's Research Group. Dr. Pinkston received a B.S. degree in electrical engineering from Princeton University in 1964. He completed his graduate studies at MIT, receiving his M.S. degree in 1966 and his Ph.D. in 1967, both in electrical engineering.

Debra M. Amidon Rogers is senior engineering manager for U.S. Sponsored Research and associate director of Digital Equipment Corporation's External Research Program, which manages relationships with 140 research centers worldwide. She has delivered papers to a wide variety of professional organizations and has published several articles and technical reports. Her professional activities span leadership in state government and national technical societies. Ms. Rogers holds degrees from Boston University and Columbia University.

Ronald G. Rosemeier is the founder and president of Brimrose Corporation of America, a scientific research and consulting company in Baltimore, Maryland. In conjunction with Johns Hopkins University, Brimrose has developed and marketed the first commercially available portable X-ray image intensifier and asymmetric crystal topographic camera. Dr. Rosemeier has published several papers in his major fields of interest, which include semiconductive materials, X-ray topography, materials analysis, nondestructive testing, and residual stress analysis. Dr. Rosemeier gained his Ph.D. from Johns Hopkins University in 1980, as well as other postgraduate degrees in mechanics and materials science at the same university.

Charles H. Shorter is vice president and general manager at TRW Information Systems Group (ISG) and is responsible for a systems integration and data base business in the commercial marketplace and for technology development and transfer to other operating units. The primary focus of Mr. Shorter's current position is new business development in the financial, telecommunications, and geographic information systems marketplace through acquisitions, alliances, and internal development. His educational background includes a B.S. degree in mathematics and an M.S. degree in systems management from the University of Southern California.

Eugene F. Stark, Jr. has served as chairman of the Federal Laboratory Consortium (FLC) since 1981. The FLC is chartered by Congress to strengthen technical cooperation between the government's 600 laboratories and the American private and public sectors. His reponsibilities include policy and program leadership for the consortium. His technical assignment at the Los Alamos National Laboratory is in radio frequency power development for the Strategic Defense Initiative. During Dr. Stark's two-year assignment to the Director's Office at Los Alamos, he was instrumental in establishing the laboratory's technology transfer program. Dr. Stark was educated at MIT in the Department of Electrical Engineering, receiving B.S. and M.S. degrees in 1969 and an Sc.D. degree in 1972.

Kathleen M. Wiltsey joined Amgen in 1984 as business development manager for Human Therapeutics. She has been active in establishing corporate partnerships, obtaining financing, working with the scientists and product development, and assessing new opportunities. Ms. Wiltsey began her career as a product development engineer at Procter & Gamble. She holds a B.S. degree in chemical engineering from the Colorado School of Mines and a master's degree from Harvard School of Business Administration.

James A. Woolley is currently technical director of 3M's Electronic Products Division, a supplier of materials, components, and systems for making electronic interconnection. He is a member of the Strategic Technology Planning Committee of 3M's Electronic and Information Technology Sector, the company's R&D management representative to MCC, and a member of 3M's Strategic Information Planning and Corporation Education Committees.

ABOUT THE SPONSORS

The RGK Foundation was established in 1966 to provide support for medical and educational research. Major emphasis has been placed on the research of connective tissue diseases, particularly sclerderma. The foundation also supports workshops and conferences at educational institutions through which the role of business in American society is examined. Such conferences have been cosponsored with the IC² Institute at the University of Texas, Austin, and with the Keystone Center in Colorado.

The RGK Foundation Building, which opened in October 1981, has a research library and provides research space for students in residence. The building's extensive conference facilities are used to conduct national and international conferences. Conferences at the RGK Foundation are designed not only to enhance information exchange on particular topics but also to maintain interlinkages between business, academia, community, and government.

Arthur Young International conducts a high-quality, worldwide practice of public accounting. Within the United States, the firm employs over 6,400 people in offices in ninety U.S. cities. Internationally, they are represented in offices in sixty-nine countries.

Financial and management consultants to the burgeoning high-technology industry, Arthur Young serves many of America's premier biotechnology companies through its High-Technology Group. It assists at every stage of business start-up in creating and implementing financing strategies and in coordinating financial strategy with business strategy.

Through the High-Technology Group, Arthur Young offers financial and accounting services to clients in biotechnology, computers, electronic peripherals, software, telecommunications, and related high-technology industries. Among the group's clients are such dynamic biotechnology enterprises as Genentech, Cetus, and Ciba-Corning Diagnostics.

The School of Business at California Polytechnic State University is composed of four departments: Accounting, Business Administration, Economics, and Management. Approximately 1,500 undergraduate students and over 150 M.B.A. students study at the School of Business. Business education at the school follows the Cal Poly tradition of skill-building, case study, problem-solving, and practical application of theory.

Cal Poly's School of Business is relatively young, having graduated its first student in 1961. The Business Administration Department expanded into a school of business as recently as 1975. Yet, a high demand for entrance to the school has led to high qualitative admission standards. The school has achieved prestige and recognition throughout California and beyond as a leading institution in business education.

California Engineering Foundation (CEF) was founded in 1974 to provide a central focus for California's technical community to deal effectively with the broad concerns facing the state that relate to engineering, science, and technology.

Of paramount interest are those challenges related to education, including career guidance; science, math, and technology literacy of school children; science- and technology-related postsecondary education with emphasis on engineering programs; engineering research; continuing education; and public understanding of science and technology. The CEF is actively involved in research and coordination of technical public policy.

Since its founding, the CEF has conducted research, convened conferences and workshops, developed expositions, assisted in technology transfer, and provided counsel and direction to industry, education, and public offices.

The California Engineering Foundation receives support from industrial firms, technical schools, individuals, and public entities. The CEF is controlled by its board of directors of policy-level individuals from industry, government, and education in California.